CONTENTS

INTRODUCTION

The work contained within this book aims to develop the children's knowledge of language and their ability to use it effectively. Ideally, the activities should take their place within the children's experience and study of whole texts, providing opportunities to focus upon aspects of grammatical interest. It is intended that teachers introduce terminology to reinforce concepts, and to stimulate an on-going interest in language. The main hope is that children will be able to use the knowledge and interest acquired to deepen their understanding of reading and become more proficient at writing; able to adapt their language to suit different situations.

Grammar is a subject about which much has been written and said in recent times. It is a subject – like spelling – which attracts media interest and political pontification. I would agree with Sue Palmer and Peter Brinton in their belief that:

> ...some time must be devoted to ensuring that children know the meaning of linguistic terminology and some of the rules that underlie the system of language. If teachers rely on 'incidental teaching' techniques exclusively (for example, explaining the characteristics of a noun only if it happens to crop up in conversation), the children's knowledge will be patchy in the extreme. However, teaching about language need not mean the 'old-fashioned grammar exercises', which Kingman (and all post-Plowden educationists) so rightly eschew.

Many of those who write about grammar teaching are swift to take up the notion that old-fashioned exercises are dull, turn children off English and hinder their ability to use language more effectively. They suggest that teachers should seek out new and interesting ways of teaching grammar. Professor Ron Carter, who headed the L.I.N.C. project which looked at knowledge about language, said recently: 'You can't turn your back on it – it needs to be faced. I am optimistic that teachers can get to grips with this quite quickly if they get their heads together to come up with interesting, exciting and flexible ways to teach grammar.' This book aims to add to the supply of material for teachers wishing to develop their grammar teaching creatively.

I have attempted to steer a course that will provide interesting activities for the children. I have not been prescriptive regarding the precise meanings of terminology. One of the major difficulties of teaching grammar is that soon the whole process of looking at words can become very complex, full of rules and exceptions to them. Indeed, every reference book I have used to research this area provides different definitions and categories for the main parts of speech.

The National Curriculum document proposes that children at Key Stages 1 and 2 should develop an interest in words, consider their effectiveness and develop their ability to use words appropriately. This book has been divided into five sections that cover: Parts of speech, Word study, Sentences, Punctuation and Record keeping. This should allow the children to acquire a 'feel' for categorising words within a simple framework, so that when discussing their own writing and the writing of others a common language may be adopted. I have also included activities to help the children savour and appreciate words and how they work together, encouraging them to consider what correct or standard English is, and for what audience this might be needed.

Standard English

English in the National Curriculum (1995) made it clear that: '...in order to participate confidently in public, cultural and working life, pupils need to be able to speak, write and read standard English fluently and accurately. All pupils are therefore entitled to the full range of opportunities necessary to enable them to develop competence in standard English.' The Orders make it clear that standard English is a dialect: '...distinguished from other forms of English by its vocabulary, and by rules and conventions of grammar, spelling and punctuation.' The Orders continue to make it clear that: '...spoken standard English is not the same as Received Pronunciation, and can be expressed in a variety of accents'.

As children begin to mature in their use of English, they become more able to adapt their writing and speech to suit the audience and purpose. In formal situations, where standard English is appropriate, pupils begin to adapt and adopt the appropriate vocabulary and grammar. As with all learning of language, the adult role model – the teacher – interacts both by demonstrating the standard form and by helping the children to refine and reconsider their use of English where it is not appropriate.

It is worth noting that it is not until Level seven in Speaking and listening that pupils are expected to '...show confident use of standard English in situations that require it'.

HOW TO USE THIS BOOK

The special focus

The teacher should only introduce an aspect of punctuation or a grammatical term when the children are ready. Begin by providing a clear explanation of the part of grammar under scrutiny – to the whole class or to a group of children. This should be followed by the use of relevant activities. The teacher should avoid introducing concepts too quickly, as this leads to confusion and loss of interest on the part of many individuals.

Using their knowledge

Once an aspect of grammar or punctuation has been introduced, it will need to be reinforced by the application of this knowledge through discussion of reading, and in the children's writing. After all, there is little point in knowing what adjectives are if you cannot use them effectively! It is therefore intended that grammar and punctuation are best taught in an interesting and varied way through the use of a planned focus, supported by further work within the children's own reading and writing. The on-going development of an interest in words is preferable to slavish adherence to dull exercises that do not relate to children's own experience of reading and writing.

Working within the National Curriculum

Although teachers will need to select material appropriate to the level and ability of their classes, the National Curriculum grid (pages viii–ix) indicates which copymasters may be more relevant to Key Stage 1 or to Key Stage 2. I would suggest that Key Stage 2 teachers read and consider easier copymasters to reinforce skills with those still operating at an earlier stage. Categorising words is a conceptual leap which many infant children are not ready to make.

HOW TO USE THE COPYMASTERS

Children develop their use of grammar through constant engagement with the language of their society. Their ability to use and manipulate conventions – such as punctuation – grows over a period of time. Through constant use, the children's language is refined in response to the language that they are surrounded by. When moving to a new area, children will often adapt their language or accent in order to fit in. The ability of children to adapt language is powerful.

All children should have access to the grammar of standard English. However, prescriptive rules may well be ineffective as a method of introducing the children to its application. It is worth remembering that before rules can be abstracted, competence must emerge. Too often in the past, children were introduced to the rules and regulations of grammar before they were ready, and so could not connect these with the ways in which they created and interpreted language. With this in mind, the copymasters have been designed to provide interactive activities that children will enjoy and find engaging.

The following points provide brief descriptions of how the copymasters can be used most effectively in the classroom situation:

1. Provide a clear explanation of the aspect of grammar or punctuation being introduced. **Demonstrate** several examples in front of the children. Usually this will mean writing in front of them. (I find a whiteboard useful for such work.)

2. It will often be necessary for the children or teacher to read examples aloud. This is important, as it is often easier to 'hear' what is correct or incorrect.

3. Create your own copymasters based on ideas found in this book. Adjust their content to the level of the children that you are working with.

4. Encourage the children to compare their work and discuss any differences.

5. Sessions may be more focused if a time limit is used to create a sense of urgency and to encourage concentration.

6. Small group work should be used wherever possible.

7. The children could invent their own copymasters to reinforce earlier work.

8. Where the children are asked to create poems or short pieces of prose and write them on to the copymaster, working drafts should be written elsewhere and the copymaster used for their final version.

9. Once an aspect of grammar or punctuation has been **demonstrated** and a copymaster used and **discussed**, the activity should be **reinforced** through the children's own reading, writing and discussion activities. For instance, an aspect of punctuation should be identified within the children's own writing, and they should be encouraged to proofread their work as well as the work of others. Also, the term which has been introduced should be the focus of a class discussion.

10. The copymasters often show the incorrect use of grammar or punctuation. These should be used to bring to the surface the children's implicit knowledge of grammar.

11. Some of the processes suggested in the copymasters could be applied in many different ways. For instance, the children could use coloured pencils to identify particular parts of speech within any text. This could be a way of introducing poems or short pieces of prose for discussion. A photocopy of a child's own work, a passage the teacher has prepared or a selected text could be used to focus upon adjectives or verbs, which can be used to add strength, extra colour or persuasion.

BOOK LIST

Books with ideas

All About English, John and Elizabeth Seely, Oxford University Press (1990).

This book is intended for Key Stage 3 children. Based on the findings of the Kingman Report, it provides an overview of how language works. This would make an ideal introductory text for teachers; it is clear, straightforward and has useful reference sections on punctuation, grammar and word play.

Inspirations for Grammar, George Hunt, Scholastic (1994).

A useful book that provides some background theory, as well as practical activities for the classroom. The book places grammar in a broad context, and includes chapters on letter-strings, words and their meanings, phrases and sentences, written texts, oral discourse, language diversity and standard English.

Word Games, Sandy Brownjohn and Janet Whitaker, Hodder and Stoughton (1985).

This is an excellent source of lively activities that encourage children to play games with language. (Also purchase *More Word Games*, the companion volume.) Sandy Brownjohn's other books on teaching poetry writing are invaluable: *Does It Have to Rhyme?*, *What Rhymes with Secret?* and *The Ability to Name Cats*.

The Oxford Guide to Word Games, Tony Augarde, Oxford University Press (1986).

This book is not intended for teachers, but it does contain every conceivable sort of word game - from charades to anagrams. This material is well worth adapting for classroom use.

Catapults and Kingfishers, Pie Corbett and Brian Moses, Oxford University Press (1986).

This book contains many ideas for poetry writing. A good number of these encourage the children to play with language. The book also provides writing formulae that can be used to practise writing sentences. *My Grandmother's Motorbike*, also published by Oxford University Press, is a valuable resource with hundreds of practical ideas and examples of story and prose writing.

Photocopiable stories and poetry

Tales, Myths and Legends, a Scholastic collection, editor: Pie Corbett, Scholastic (1994).

A collection of 60 storytellers' favourite tales. Most of the book is photocopiable, and therefore it is an excellent resource for classroom use. (*Poetry*, editor: Wes Magee, in the same Scholastic collections series is also a useful source of photocopiable poetry.)

Source books

The Oxford English Dictionary
Roget's Thesaurus
The Poet's Manual and Rhyming Dictionary, Francis Stillman
Brewer's Dictionary of Phrase and Fable, Cassell

Teacher's in-service material

L.I.N.C. (Language In the National Curriculum): Materials for Professional Development (1992). This is available from the L.I.N.C. secretary, Department of English Studies, University of Nottingham.

These are the in-service materials that the Government banned from publication. They provide a rigorous and academic resource to supplement the teacher's own study of linguistics. There is a good section on grammar and a technical glossary.

Curriculum coverage

This book provides coverage of all the grammar and punctuation requirements for the curricula for England and Wales, Scotland and Northern Ireland. We have set out on the following pages, in short-hand form, the key punctuation and study of language points from the Programmes of Study of each curriculum, and indicated where to go to find activities which specifically relate to these points. Of course, much of the curriculum requirement for language study work is too general to be defined by tickable points, and it is hoped that you will range widely over the activities in this book when seeking to interpret the directives of your curriculum.

Programme of study for England and Wales

Programme of study for Key Stage 1

Copymaster numbers

Punctuation

■ use capital letters	72, 81, 82, 83, 84, 85, 86, 87, 89, 91, 92, 103, 104, 105, 106, 107, 108, 114, 115, 118, 119, 120, 126
■ use full stops	81, 82, 83, 84, 85, 86, 87, 89, 91, 92, 103, 104, 105, 106, 107
■ use question marks	109, 110, 111, 112, 113, 126
■ begin to use commas	115, 116

Standard English and language study

■ introduce the vocabulary, grammar and structures of written standard English, especially	
– subject/verb agreement	33, 34
– 'to be' in past and present tense	31, 32
■ develop an understanding of sentences and word order	10, 26, 28, 31, 32, 42, 43, 50, 51, 52, 84, 86, 87, 88, 94, 103, 105, 107, 108, 109, 110, 111, 116, 126
■ ways of linking sentences together	42, 43, 44, 45
■ develop an interest in words and meanings:	
– words with similar meanings	67, 78
– opposites	62
– words with more than one meaning	—

Programme of study for Key Stage 2

Punctuation

■ use full stops	42, 46, 81, 82, 83, 84, 85, 89, 90, 91, 92, 94, 96, 97, 98, 99, 100, 101, 102, 103, 104, 105, 106, 108, 109, 122, 123, 126, 129, 131
■ use question marks	109, 110, 111, 112, 113, 126
■ use exclamation marks	126
■ use commas	98, 99, 100, 101, 102, 103, 115, 116, 117, 108, 130, 131, 127, 128
■ use inverted commas	127, 128
■ use apostrophes to mark possession	125
■ differentiate between spoken and written forms	93, 95, 31
■ different degrees of formality in written English	95, 97, 98, 99, 100
■ the grammar of complex sentences, including clauses and phrases	—
■ use paragraphs	130
■ link sentences	42, 43, 44, 45, 46

- use standard written forms of
  - nouns
  - verbs

  - adjectives
  - adverbs
  - prepositions
  - conjunctions
  - verb tenses
  - distinguish between words of similar meaning
  - explain meanings
  - experiment with vocabulary choices

  - discussion of language use and choices

nouns	1, 2, 3, 4, 6, 7, 8, 9, 10, 11, 12, 13, 16, 21, 53, 54, 55, 70, 84, 118
verbs	25, 26, 27, 28, 29, 30, 31, 32, 33, 34, 35, 36, 37, 53, 54, 55, 84, 94, 102, 101
adjectives	17, 18, 19, 20, 21, 22, 23, 24, 54, 55, 84, 102, 101, 118
adverbs	38, 39, 40, 41, 101
prepositions	47, 48, 49, 53
conjunctions	42, 43, 44, 45
verb tenses	31, 32, 33, 34
distinguish	67, 78
explain meanings	36, 38, 43, 64, 73, 79, 100, 102
experiment with vocabulary choices	6, 7, 8, 11, 12, 13, 14, 19, 20, 21, 22, 23, 24, 26, 27, 28, 29, 30, 35, 36, 37, 40, 41, 44, 45, 49, 53, 55, 58, 59, 74, 75, 76, 78, 110, 118
discussion of language use and choices	6, 7, 8, 12, 14, 18, 22, 24, 25, 26, 27, 31, 33, 37, 38, 40, 41, 44, 53, 59, 79, 82, 86, 95, 96, 97, 99, 101, 102, 110, 126, 127

Programme of study for Scotland

Relevant Programmes of study for English Language 5–14

Level A   **Copymaster numbers**

- Learn that capitals and full stops make meaning clearer

103, 105, 106

Level B

- Use full stops and capitals

72, 81, 82, 83, 84, 85, 86, 87, 89, 91, 92, 103, 104, 105, 106, 107, 108, 114, 115, 118, 119, 120, 126, 42, 46, 90, 94, 96, 97, 98, 99, 100, 101, 102, 109, 122, 123, 129, 131

- Link sentences with appropriate words

42, 43, 44, 45

- Use terms:
  - letter   —
  - word   —
  - capital   —
  - full stop   —
  - sentence   —

Level C

- Use
  - commas

98, 99, 100, 101, 102, 103, 115, 116, 117, 107, 108, 130, 131, 127, 128

  - question marks

109, 110, 111, 112, 113, 126

- Introduce paragraphing

130

- Use terms:
  - noun   —
  - verb   —
  - comma   —
  - question mark   —

Level D

- Developing paragraphing — —
- Develop sentence structure — 10, 24, 26, 28, 31, 32, 34, 42, 43, 50, 51, 52, 53, 54, 55, 81, 82, 84, 86, 87, 88, 90, 94, 103, 105, 106, 108, 109, 110, 111, 116, 117, 122, 123, 125, 126, 127, 128
- Teach direct speech — 127, 128
- Use terms:
  - vowel — —
  - consonant — —
  - adjective — —
  - pronoun — —
  - conjunction — —
  - masculine and feminine — —
  - singular and plural — —
  - tense — —

Programme of study for Northern Ireland

Programme of study for Key Stage 1

Copymaster numbers

- Write correctly structured sentences — 10, 26, 28, 31, 32, 42, 43, 50, 51, 52, 84, 86, 87, 88, 94, 103, 105, 106, 108, 109, 110, 111, 116, 126
- Use capital letters — 72, 81, 82, 83, 84, 85, 86, 87, 89, 91, 92, 103, 104, 105, 106, 107, 108, 114, 115, 118, 119, 120, 126
- Use full stops — 81, 82, 83, 84, 85, 86, 87, 89, 91, 92, 103, 104, 105, 106, 107,
- Use question marks — 109, 110, 111, 112, 113, 126
- Experiment with words through word games — 1, 3, 5, 16, 17, 21, 38, 53, 56, 57, 68, 69, 70, 71, 72, 74, 109, 111, 118

Programme of study for Key Stage 2

- Develop use of:
  - full stops — 42, 46, 81, 82, 83, 84, 85, 89, 90, 91, 92, 94, 96, 97, 98, 99, 100, 101, 102, 103, 104, 105, 106, 108, 109, 122, 123, 126
  - commas — 127, 128
  - question marks — 109, 110, 112, 113, 126
  - exclamation marks — 126
- Introduce apostrophes — 124, 125
- Function of the paragraph — 130
- Introduce direct speech — 127, 128
- Use of connectives and pronouns to avoid repetition — 42, 43, 44, 45, 50
- Experiment with verbal play and dialect — 63, 64, 76, 77, 79, 80, 93, 94, 95

PARTS OF SPEECH

This section introduces the children to the idea of categorising words and developing a shared vocabulary with which to accomplish this. Each category is introduced by teacher's notes explaining relevant terminology. A range of teaching strategies are provided, including a variety of interactive games and texts. The main aim of this approach is to develop the children's ability to: reflect on language, use it effectively and gain an understanding of how words work within sentences.

Teachers will need to build on the children's implicit understanding of grammatical rules, and encourage them to become interested in how language works. Once an aspect of language has been focused upon, it is important to reinforce this through the children's experiences as readers and writers.

Some of the copymasters may be 'corrected' straight on to the sheet, or you may wish the children to copy out passages and sentences after they have proofread them.

NOUNS

Copymaster 1 (Name that noun)
Use this copymaster to reinforce the notion that **nouns** are words that **name** things. Before giving the copymaster to the children, ask them to point to and name classroom objects, or play a game of 'I spy'. Afterwards, the children should write in the name of each item on the sheet. Emphasise that each item they name is a noun. They could then cut out and sort the illustrations into categories under the headings: animals, plants and objects. Encourage them to draw or list further nouns in these categories.

Copymaster 2 (Nouns all around)
Use this copymaster as a reinforcement activity. The children – alone or in pairs – should identify as many nouns as they can in the picture and list these in the space provided. This process could be repeated using posters or any other form of illustration.

Copymaster 3 (The shopping alphabet)
This is a version of the old game where children sit in a circle and take it in turns to relate what they have bought on a shopping trip. Introduce the copymaster by playing this game. The first child only has to name one item, whilst others add to the list and recall what previous people have said. The last person has the task of remembering what everyone has 'bought'! Afterwards, ask the children to write an alphabetical shopping list on the copymaster (dictionaries may be useful). Emphasise the idea that each item listed is a noun.

Copymaster 4 (Little and large)
This copymaster further reinforces the concept of 'naming words'. The children should draw and label things that are: smaller than a matchbox, smaller than a dog but bigger than a matchbox, larger than a car.

Copymaster 5 (Male or female?)
The children cut out and sort the pictures into males and females. They could then paste each group on to a separate piece of paper and colour and label them. Afterwards, provide the children with further drawings, lists or cuttings from magazines to sort. Alternatively, invent quizzes where they are asked the male or female names for various creatures or occupations.

Copymaster 6 (The alphabetical party)
This copymaster reinforces alphabetical order and the children's work on nouns. They should complete the guest list of 'occupation' nouns (the first two have been done for them). It might be best if groups or the whole class brainstormed ideas before individuals complete the sheet. Emphasise that the 'guests' can be as weird and wonderful as they like.

Copymaster 7 (Sausages?)
This could be the opening passage of a typical fairy story. However, all the nouns have been removed and replaced with the word **sausage(s)**. Ask the children to read the passage, or read it aloud yourself. At first offer no clues and see if they can begin to find appropriate nouns to replace the word **sausage(s)**. The children should then cross out the word **sausage(s)** each time it appears and write these nouns over the top. The children could compare final versions to see if they make sense.

Copymaster 8 (Not a noun in sight)
All the nouns have been removed from this passage. The children should read it aloud and then, as a group or in pairs, insert appropriate nouns. Final versions should then be compared for sense.

Copymaster 9 (Vice versa)
Ask the children to cross out the various nouns and swap their gender – male for female and vice versa.

1

Copymaster 10 (Local news)
The children should change the singular nouns (in bold) to plural where sensible and possible. This activity aims to highlight the fact that sometimes making nouns plural affects other words in the sentence or passage, that need altering as a result. Afterwards, the children could write lists of nouns and their plurals (they may need to use dictionaries).

Copymaster 11 (Name that group)
This set of collective nouns could act as a reference point for further work. Ask the children to add to the list and then invent new collective nouns for the groups given or for other nouns (for example, a tiredness of teachers, a chaos of children, a relic of folders). They should then complete each phrase, for example:
– A pack of wolves **waits wearily**.
– A school of whales **wallows wonderfully**.
– A pride of lions lies **in wait**.

Copymaster 12 (New groups)
The children should invent collective nouns which relate to the items shown on the copymaster. For example, a **chaos** of cars. It might be useful for the children to brainstorm answers in groups.

Copymaster 13 (What are they called?)
This copymaster is in two sections. In the first section, collective nouns need to be added; these could be the traditional nouns associated with these groups or the children could invent their own. In the second section,

the nouns themselves are missing; again they could insert the traditional nouns, or make intelligent guesses. This sheet might be used for homework. Ask the children to discover as many collective nouns as possible, which could be used to complete each of the passages.

Copymaster 14 (Space story)
This copymaster introduces proper nouns. Explain that they name something special: people, places, days of the week, months, seasons, special days, planets and stars. Emphasise that they must begin with a capital letter.

The copymaster could be filled in by pairs or individuals using appropriate nouns. The children should check each other's 'space stories' to see if they make sense and to make sure that all the proper nouns begin with a capital letter.

Copymaster 15 (Proper nouns)
The children could complete this task on their own or in groups. They should plan a journey (using an atlas) and fill in the travel agent's 'information sheet'. Remind them to use capital letters for all the proper nouns.

Copymaster 16 (The naming game)
This activity combines the children's work on nouns and proper nouns. It can be used as a timed game or a set piece of homework. The children should complete an alphabetical list under each of the headings. Their work should be checked to see if they have used capital letters appropriately.

ADJECTIVES

Copymaster 17 (What do they look like?)
The children should list as many 'describing words' as they can think of for each of the illustrations in the boxes. Explain that these are **adjectives**. An **adjective describes** a noun. This activity could be carried out by small groups in a timed situation. Which group can discover the largest number of adjectives? Extend the activity by playing a game. The children sit in a circle and take it in turns to say a noun to their neighbour, who has to think of an appropriate adjective to go with it.

Copymaster 18 (Silly adjectives)
The children should read through the passage carefully and look at the picture. Some of the adjectives seem to have been muddled up. The children need to change them around to match what is happening in the picture – they may need some help. The passage could be corrected or rewritten. Afterwards, the children could compare their results.

Copymaster 19 (The headteacher's dog)
This is the 'Minister's cat' in a different guise. The children complete the alphabetical list of words to describe the dog (a dictionary may be needed). Introduce this activity by completing several examples in front of the children. For example, the headteacher's dog is: an **amiable** dog that licks your hand, a **bright** dog that likes a bone, a **cool** dog that lies in the shade. The

class could then use this idea for other lists, for example the headteacher's parrot is …

Copymaster 20 (Nonsense adjectives)
The children should replace the made-up adjectives with those that they feel are more appropriate. The invented adjectives should be underlined and then crossed out. Improvements could be written above the text or the sentences rewritten. Extend the activity by asking the children to invent adjectives for each other to use. They could give a list of five adjectives to a friend, who has to write a mini-saga of 50 words using all of them.

Copymaster 21 (Crazy combinations)
This copymaster has a column of adjectives and a column of nouns. The idea is to identify 'possible' combinations and to write sentences using them. This sort of work reinforces the 'nature' of adjectives in a fun way – using them inappropriately. Afterwards, the children could add more words to each column for further 'crazy combinations'.

Copymaster 22 (Autumn)
This is a poetic description. Ask the children to write appropriate adjectives in the spaces provided. Emphasise that they should try to avoid repetition and

not use the first idea that comes into their heads (a thesaurus might be useful). Afterwards, discuss their selection of words.

Copymaster 23 (Summer morning)
This poem has too many adjectives. The children should work on the sheet selecting the adjective in each line which they think is best and crossing out the others. Afterwards, the children should read the poem aloud to see if they made the 'right' choices.

Copymaster 24 (The ring)
There are no adjectives in this passage. In pairs, the children could read it through and then insert suitable adjectives in appropriate places. For example: 'They peered down the (narrow) road and could see nothing but (dark) shadows.' The final versions should be read aloud and compared to see which create an exciting atmosphere most effectively and communicate a clear picture to the reader. Encourage the children to continue the story using the same style of writing.

VERBS

Copymaster 25 (The great verb list)
This copymaster will need to be discussed before the children begin. Explain that verbs tell us what is happening in a sentence. They **describe** the **action.** Without a verb the sentence is dead.

The children should write words that describe actions (verbs or 'doing words') on the page near to the relevant parts of the body. For example, by the head they could write: shake, nod, turn, look, stare, glare, peer, talk, chatter, gossip, giggle, snigger. The idea of verbs being introduced through actions could be applied during a gym session focusing upon different ways of moving.

Copymaster 26 (What do they do?)
These incomplete sentences should be read aloud to the class so they can hear what it sounds like when a verb is missing. Let the children read them aloud to each other. The activity involves a simple cloze procedure – the children fill the gaps with verbs. Comparison and discussion of the verbs used is important as some choices will be more effective than others.

Copymaster 27 (Monkey verbs)
This is a very popular copymaster because it sounds so funny. Encourage the children to read the text aloud, as this will help them to gain a sense of the events taking place. The word **monkey** has to be crossed out and a suitable verb written above to replace it. The children's choices of verbs should then be compared and discussed. Afterwards, ask the children to write a paragraph approximately ten lines long. Each verb should be rubbed out and the word monkey (or some other word) inserted. The children should then swap pieces of work and add suitable verbs. Avoid the idea of a 'right' answer. Allow the children to consider a range of possibilities.

Copymaster 28 (Wanted – verbs!)
These incomplete sentences should be read aloud. Ask the children to write an appropriate verb in the correct position in each sentence – the whole sentence may be rewritten or the verb inserted in the space above. The children should grasp the idea, that generally speaking, a sentence should have a verb. The verb gives the sentence its life.

Copymaster 29 (Verb poem)
To complete this 'two-word poem' (which could run into two columns) the children need a list of names. They should add verbs to these to describe what the children are doing. Encourage them to make their poems rhyme.

Copymaster 30 (Making sense)
Encourage the children to read the passage aloud. They should then identify, cross out and replace the verbs with more suitable alternatives. Afterwards, suggest that they create their own silly verb poems or stories.

Copymaster 31 (Teddy talk)
As the children mature as writers, they will need to be able to identify and use the correct form of the verb to be. This can present difficulties as this verb is often used incorrectly in everyday speech. Highlight and discuss this problem before the children begin the copymaster. They should read aloud the sentences in the speech bubbles and then correct them. Afterwards, they should read the sentences aloud again to ensure that they make sense.

Copymaster 32 (To be)
This copymaster reinforces work on the verb to be. The children have to make the verb agree with the rest of the sentence. Maintaining the correct and regular use of tenses is something children need to be aware of in their own writing.

Copymaster 33 (Stop, thief!)
The passage should be rewritten in the past tense (in the space provided). This may reveal whether certain children are aware of spelling conventions. For example, a word like 'grab' will have a double 'b' in the past tense. However, the passage contains many exceptions to such basic conventions, and these should be highlighted and discussed before the children begin the activity.

Copymaster 34 (Feeding time at the zoo)
This copymaster emphasises the importance of ensuring that the subject and verb agree. The children should read the sentences aloud, and on their own or in pairs alter the verbs. Encourage them to examine pieces of their own written work to see if they have made similar mistakes and can correct them.

Copymaster 35 (Name it!)
On this copymaster I have replaced key verbs with animals' names. Of course, some animals' names have been turned into verbs (for example, pigging yourself) to describe actions that relate to the animal. Read the passage aloud and ask the children to insert more

appropriate verbs. They could then write or copy out a passage or poem and replace the existing verbs with new ones that originate from the names of animals, flowers, trees, people or places. This sort of work is interesting, amusing and helps the children to identify a certain category of words.

Copymaster 36 (Nonsense verbs)
The children should continue making up sentences with invented verbs in them. Encourage them to illustrate the verbs, as shown, to demonstrate their

meaning. They could swap their work with a friend who has to find a verb that makes sense in the context.

Copymaster 37 (Stormy night)
All the verbs have been removed from this poem. Initially, the children could work on this activity alone, then in pairs and afterwards in groups of four, to share ideas. Emphasise that the idea is not just to fill in the gaps but to make up an effective poem with strong verbs. Reading their work aloud will help the children to hear how effective the chosen words are.

ADVERBS

Copymaster 38 (The great adverb hunt)
Before the children begin the copymaster, discuss adverbs. Adverbs describe **how** actions are carried out. They **add** to the **verb** informing us about the quality of actions. They often end in 'ly'.

A useful introduction to adverbs is to play 'In the manner of the word'. One child is sent out of the room. Everyone else agrees on an adverb, let us say they choose 'slowly'. The child returns to the room and has to guess the word. The child does this by asking class members to perform certain actions in the manner of the word. So, a child might be asked to sing, and has to do this slowly. The child then guesses the word and if s/he is wrong takes another turn.

The copymaster requires that the children write as many adverbs as they can that are relevant to the illustrated actions.

Copymaster 39 (Lazy adverbs)
One or two adverbs are chosen and a list poem written.

The copymaster provides an example of this. The children could write their final draft of the poem in the space provided on the copymaster.

Copymaster 40 (Nice one!)
Almost every teacher becomes irritated with children's tendency to over-use the word 'nice'. Challenge the children to swap every 'nicely' on the copymaster for an alternative adverb. It might be useful for groups of children to brainstorm suitable adverbs.

Copymaster 41 (Building a glider)
This copymaster involves a simple cloze procedure. The children should begin by reading the passage aloud, perhaps making a noise or saying some other word in the gaps. The children should then fill in the gaps using suitable adverbs. Afterwards, discuss the adverbs that they have chosen.

CONJUNCTIONS

Copymaster 42 (Because)
Conjunctions **connect** parts of sentences. Children often over-use the conjunctions 'and' and 'then' when they write. In part this is because they are focusing upon the sequence of a plot, and they do not read their own writing objectively. They need to be shown how to insert full stops or use alternative conjunctions when appropriate. Demonstrate how to position full stops in one or two instances, using the children's own written work, and then send the children off to make further improvements. For example, say: "I can see three other places where you could replace an 'and'. Go and see if you can."

The copymaster shows a poem that uses the alternating phrases – I like … because … and I do not like … because …. Demonstrate how to complete similar phrases, for example, I like cows because they chew grass, or, I do not like silence because it scares me. The children should then fill in the gaps on the copymaster and use the space provided to continue the poem in the same style.

Copymaster 43 (Secrets)
This poem needs to be completed, providing the

children with the opportunity to practise using the conjunction 'but'. The session could begin with the children swapping secrets and inventing new secrets. Read through the beginning of the poem with them. Then, invent some new lines as a group. The children should write their first draft elsewhere and use the copymaster for their final version – having checked the spelling, grammar and punctuation. The children could then illustrate each line.

Copymaster 44 (A good excuse?)
The children should complete the sentences. Point out that each conjunction has a slightly different shade of meaning. Encourage them to write impossible and wonderful excuses, for example: 'I would have been early but a passing, flying badger swooped down and took me home for tea.' The finished products could be shared and discussed.

Copymaster 45 (A bad day)
The children select conjunctions from those listed at the bottom of the page to fill in the gaps. Emphasise that there is no one 'right' answer.

Copymaster 46 (Conjunctions)
The child who wrote this passage used 'and'/'then' far too often. The children could rewrite the passage or simply proofread it and make improvements. Afterwards, encourage them to complete the story.

PREPOSITIONS

Copymaster 47 (Spot the duck)
A **preposition** tells the reader **where** a noun is placed. A preposition comes before a noun, connecting it to the rest of the sentence. Introduce this category of words with a physical demonstration, using a box and a ball. The children should say one word to describe where the ball is when the teacher places it: **on**, **in**, **beside**, **behind** the box. Explain that these words are prepositions.

The copymaster requires that the children select prepositions to describe where the duck is in each picture and write them in the spaces provided.

Copymaster 48 (Where is the cat?)
The children should look at the picture and formulate a series of phrases describing where the cat is (using the prepositions at the bottom of the copymaster). For example, the cat could be: **in** the dustbin, **on** the fence, **between** two other cats.

Copymaster 49 (Position poem)
This sheet acts as an example. The children should read it and then write their own 'position poem'. Choose a setting, for example, a circus, zoo, shop, school or kitchen and ask them to use a different preposition to begin each line. Another method would be for them to use the same preposition at the start of each line, for example:

Above the mountains the clouds drift,
above the sea the seagulls skim,
above the tarmac road the heat shimmers.

PRONOUNS AND ARTICLES

Copymaster 50 (Pronouns)
Read aloud the passage at the top of the copymaster. This makes it quite clear how useful pronouns can be; they **take the place** of **nouns** and help to avoid this kind of repetition. The activity below is a cloze procedure. The children 'read' through the passage and fill in the gaps using the common pronouns listed at the bottom of the page.

Copymaster 51 (Whose skates?)
Ask the children to select the correct possessive pronoun for each circumstance from the list provided. They should then rewrite the passage in the space provided. The children need to learn how to use possessive pronouns effectively. Reinforce the idea that **its** (possessive) has no apostrophe. **It's** that means **it is** has an apostrophe.

Copymaster 52 (Escape!)
Articles are the smallest category of words – **a**, **an**, **the**. Explain to the children that we use these **before** nouns. Before a noun which begins with a vowel we use **an** rather than **a**. The copymaster provides an opportunity to reinforce this convention. The children should fill in the gaps with the correct form of the article and complete the sentences imaginatively using conjunctions. Read the following examples, invent some sentences together and then challenge the children to write their own:

– Catch an ant and watch it juggle with bananas.
– Catch an eel and watch it read the weather forecast.
– Catch a bear and listen to it whistle 'Mary had a little lamb'.

REINFORCEMENT ACTIVITIES

Copymaster 53 (Cut-up sentences)
This is a game that allows the children to manipulate the elements of sentences to create new sentences. Cut out and glue the four headings on to a separate piece of paper. Then, cut out the other boxes with words inside them. Demonstrate how nouns which appear at the end of a sentence can also be used at the beginning. Provide the children with their own copymasters and ask them to find out whether: a sentence can start with a preposition or a verb. Encourage the children to experiment further. Can they make longer sentences? Are other words needed? What sort of words are they?

Copymaster 54 (Spot the word)
This is a particularly effective way of reinforcing categories of words. Using three different-coloured crayons, the children should underline or circle nouns, adjectives and verbs. Remind them of the different categories before they start the activity. Afterwards, suggest that they finish the story. This type of activity could be repeated using many of the copymasters in this book.

Copymaster 55 (Consequences)
Provide each child with a copymaster. They should write eight adjectives in the first column. This is then folded over. They pass their copymaster to another person who writes a list of eight nouns in the second column, and the process continues until all the columns are completed. The copymaster is then handed back to the original child, who should try to make sentences from the words. These could be used to generate stories or poems.

Name _____

Name that noun

Name _____

Nouns all around

Nouns

Name _____

The shopping alphabet

I went to the shop and I bought:

a _____   o _____

b _____   p _____

c _____   q _____

d _____   r _____

e _____   s _____

f _____   t _____

g _____   u _____

h _____   v _____

i _____   w _____

j _____   x _____

k _____   y _____

l _____   z _____

m _____

n _____

Copymaster 3

Larger than a ...	Smaller than a ...	Smaller than a ...

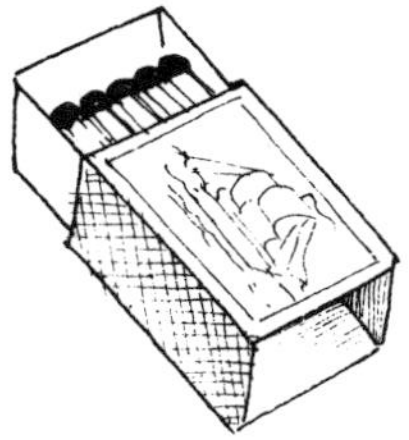

Little and large

Male or female?

Name ______________________________

The alphabetical party

Ladies and gentlemen, please welcome:

a An **a**rtist waving a brush

b A **b**urglar complete with cat

c

d

e

f

g

h

i

j

k

l

m

n

o

p

q

r

s

t

u

v

w

x

y

z

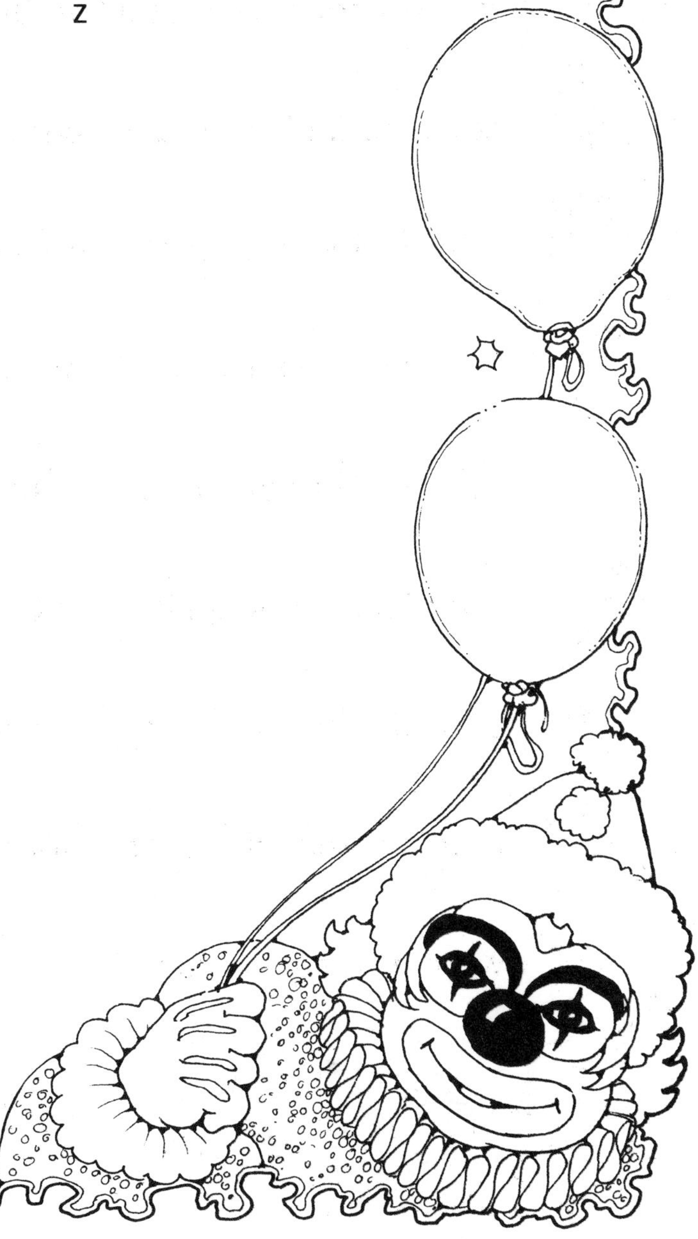

Sausages?

Once upon a sausage there lived a little old sausage.

This little old sausage lived in a dark sausage. She

used to feed the woodland sausages with sausage

and sausage. One day two evil sausages came to the

sausage and started to scare the sausages away. The

old sausage found out. She picked up her sausage

and ran down to where the sausages were camping.

She caught hold of one of them and said, "Now, get

out of our sausage and leave us alone or I'll smack

you with my sausage." The evil sausages were afraid

of this fierce little old sausage and ran away. They

were never seen again.

Name _____

Not a noun in sight

I woke up this _____ and saw that my

_____ had been stolen. I pulled on my _____ and ran

down the _____. My _____ was nowhere to be seen.

Someone had stolen it for sure. I ran down the _____ and

looked everywhere. In the _____ I could see a _____ just

like mine. Two _____ were pushing it up the _____. I

ran towards them shouting and yelling. One of the _____

turned round. He saw me and began to run. He leaped over a

_____ and ran across someone's back _____. I ran

after him but slipped into a _____. I was wet through and had a

_____ on my _____. When the _____ of the

_____ came out he was not too pleased. I explained that I had

been chasing two _____.

Copymaster 8

Name _____

Vice versa

The landlord waved goodbye to the young girl as she mounted her

stallion. Her grandfather stood at the gate waving a handkerchief.

Would he ever see his granddaughter again?

She rode through the farmyard and past the hens, the pea-hens, the

sow and the old gander. From the woods the vixen saw the young

girl ride past the shepherdess. She rode on towards the distant

castle where a strange group waited for her. On the castle walls

stood the old king, the young prince and the young tailoress.

LOCAL NEWS

GRAND OPENING!

The new **arcade** on Smith Street is now open! Leave the bustle of the **pavement** and the roar of the **car** and rush in. The **shop** is crammed with a **gift**.

Here you can buy anything you fancy – from a **computer** to a **cuddly toy**. Even the **baby** can be kept happy at the new **Punch and Judy stall**. At the **supermarket**, you can buy a **potato, tomato** and even a **piano**! So do not do a thing by half. Drop in and spend a **penny**!

Name that group

a **pack** of wolves

a **school** of whales

a **pride** of lions

a **flight** of planes

a **forest** of trees

a **swarm** of bees

a **library** of books

a **gaggle** of geese

a **suit** of clothes

a **set** of fingerprints

a **rope** of pearls

a **plague** of locusts

a **batch** of bread

a **herd** of buffaloes

a **cluster** of stars

a **flight** of swallows

a **clutch** of eggs

a **tuft** of grass

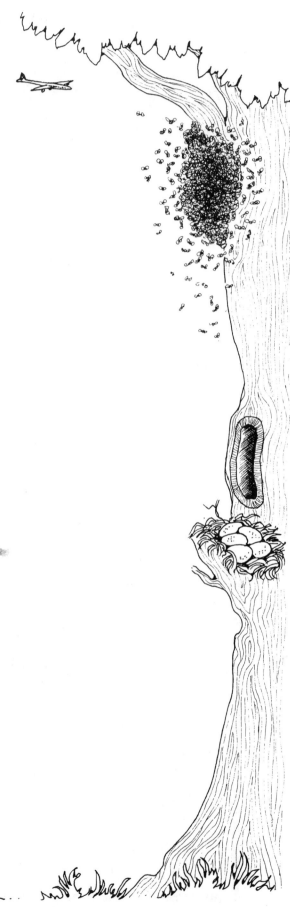

Name _____

New groups

_____

_____

_____

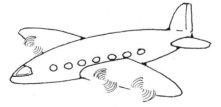

_____

_____

_____

Name _____

What are they called?

Tom stopped and stared. He was in the most

enormous zoo. Ahead of him he could see a

_____ of wolves, a _____ of lions,

a _____ of chickens, a _____ of

cattle, a _____ of bees, a _____ of

birds, a _____ of rabbits, a _____ of

pups, a _____ of monkeys, a _____

of chicks, a _____ of elephants, a

_____ of fish, a _____ of deer

and a _____ of piglets.

I ran into the market square. I could see a company of

_____ , a gang of _____ , a staff of

_____ , a board of _____ , an

audience of _____ , a crowd of _____ ,

a team of _____ , a party of _____ , a

band of _____ and a crew of _____ .

Name _____

Space story

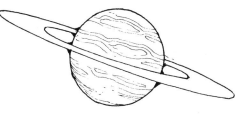

It was in the month of _____, 1999, when the first intergalactic

space cruiser reached the distant planet of _____. It was

launched from the country of _____. The launch pad was in

the unknown town of _____. At daybreak on the first

_____ of _____ , the townsfolk awoke to the noise of

the spacecruiser leaving. The noise of the launch was so loud and the

blast so bright that sightings of the cruiser were reported in

_____. The cruiser was named after its inventor _____.

The cruiser was manned by three astronauts _____ ,

_____ and Commander _____.

Proper nouns

HOLLY DAYS TRAVEL AGENCY

Names and addresses of passengers:

Country of destination: _____

Special places you wish to visit:

• Towns or cities: _____

_____

• Mountains: _____

_____

• Rivers: _____

_____

• Seas: _____

_____

• Other places of interest: _____

Name of the airport you wish to leave from: _____

The naming game

	Girls' names	Boys' names	Animals	Place names
a				
b				
c				
d				
e				
f				
g				
h				
i				
j				
k				
l				
m				
n				
o				
p				
q				
r				
s				
t				
u				
v				
w				
x				
y				
z				

What do they look like?

Silly adjectives

The angry stranger had a tall dog. He had been sitting under a tiny tree until he saw the frightened snake by the tiny tower. The evil stranger got up and ran away.

Name _____

The headteacher's dog

The headteacher's dog is

a _____

b _____

c _____

d _____

e _____

f _____

g _____

h _____

i _____

j _____

k _____

l _____

m _____

n _____

o _____

p _____

q _____

r _____

s _____

t _____

u _____

v _____

w _____

x _____

y _____

z _____

Nonsense adjectives

1. The grook knife cut through the toor vegetables.

2. The fash salmon dived into the wrat river.

3. The drog serpent slithered towards the hilth princess.

4. The parge moon shone down on the furt town.

5. He tugged on his gids helmet and drove to the wask city.

6. I picked a kirt blade of fid grass and chewed it.

7. My knees were dort and kidge after netball.

8. The tower block is so jook that you can hardly see the top.

9. I stared into the hast flames and wished.

10. The genie opened its grooked mouth and giggled.

Name _____

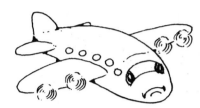

Crazy combinations

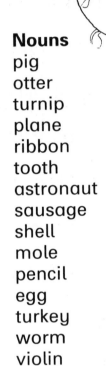

Adjectives	**Nouns**
thick	pig
thin	otter
fierce	turnip
sad	plane
busy	ribbon
honest	tooth
heavy	astronaut
wise	sausage
angry	shell
smooth	mole
pale	pencil
crisp	egg
narrow	turkey
sturdy	worm
hasty	violin

Copymaster 21

Autumn

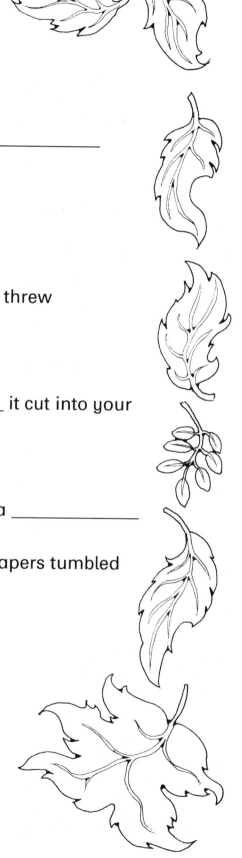

An autumn morning.

The _____ sun shone.

In the _____ hedges the spider's _____

web glistened with _____ dew.

The _____ leaves drifted down.

The _____ wind picked them up and threw

_____ handfuls into the air.

The _____ air was so _____ it cut into your

_____ face.

The _____ starlings quarrelled over a _____

scrap in the gutter and _____ newspapers tumbled

down the _____ road.

_____ cars cruised by.

The _____ milk van rattled by.

Summer morning

Shiny, glittery diamond dew on the fresh rose

bushes sparkles in the bright, hot sunshine.

Multi-coloured, blue, yellow, frail, fragile butterflies

dither and dodge in mid-air.

A slow, green, noisy, tiny car climbs the steep,

long, tall hill.

White, distant, gentle, soft clouds are like pillows

stuffed with dreams.

The bold, blustery, sharp, cruel wind sleeps.

Fat, busy, bees murmur.

The soft, calm, sleepy, tired, warm cat snoozes on

the red, flat, uneven, old brick wall.

Copymaster 23

The ring

They peered down the road and could see nothing but shadows.

The children squatted down behind the dustbin and waited. The

street lights flickered on. A cat rummaged through the scraps in the

gutter. A lady stopped to ask the children if they were alright. Her

hand shook as she bent down to talk to them. In her hand she held a

ring. The ring glowed. She smiled at them and they knew that she

was the one they should follow. A car passed them and they

thought they saw the faces of the Guardians. "Wait," said the lady.

She raised her hand and pointed her finger. There was a crack of

light and ...

The great verb list

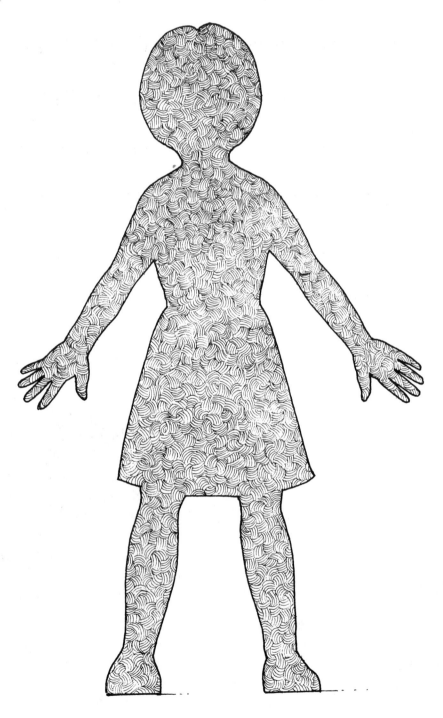

Copymaster 25

What do they do?

1. The carpenter _____ nails into the door.

2. The model _____ her fingernails.

3. The pilot _____ the plane over the hills.

4. The dentist _____ our teeth.

5. My mum makes me _____ my teeth every night.

6. The fishermen _____ in a net full of silver fish.

7. The newsagent _____ while he waits for a customer.

8. The doctor _____ to my heart-beat.

9. The dancer _____ on the tips of her toes.

10. The teacher _____ at her class when

they are quiet.

Name _____

Monkey verbs

The school girl monkeyed down the road monkeyed by the dog.

The dog monkeyed and monkeyed up at her.

The dog monkeyed into her ankle.

She monkeyed for help.

A postman monkeyed up to help her.

The postman monkeyed at the dog.

"That dog is dangerous," he monkeyed.

Along monkeyed a white van.

Two men in overalls monkeyed out.

They monkeyed the dog with a pole and a net.

They monkeyed the dog into the van.

They monkeyed away.

Wanted – verbs!

1. The dog down the hill.

2. If I you that again you in trouble.

3. The white whale beneath the ocean.

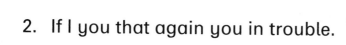

4. Corgis the Queen's favourite dogs.

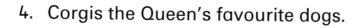

5. Milk from cows and goats good for us.

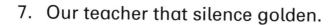

6. Gerbils from the desert.

7. Our teacher that silence golden.

8. My writing very untidy.

9. You in my way.

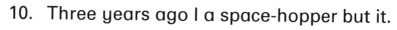

10. Three years ago I a space-hopper but it.

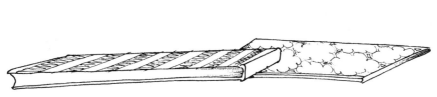

Copymaster 28

Verb poem

In the playground you can see:

Tom runs,

Janet hums,

Brian shakes,

Susie brakes,

Tracy sings,

Billy flings,

Shazzy sneezes,

Gazzer breezes,

Making sense

I juggled up early this morning and quickly got wriggled. I mowed

on my pullover as it was cold. I wrinkled down the stairs and

sniggered up my breakfast. Mum froze me to eat properly. At the

back of the house I feel up the bank and forgot down the road. My

friend Sally was weaving for me. She collapsed me a sweet and we

forgot a toffee each. We threw the bus to school. It walked down the

High Street. We munched off at the coffee shop and whispered the last

bit to school. "Boil here," knelt Mr Jones. It soaked like trouble for us.

Teddy talk

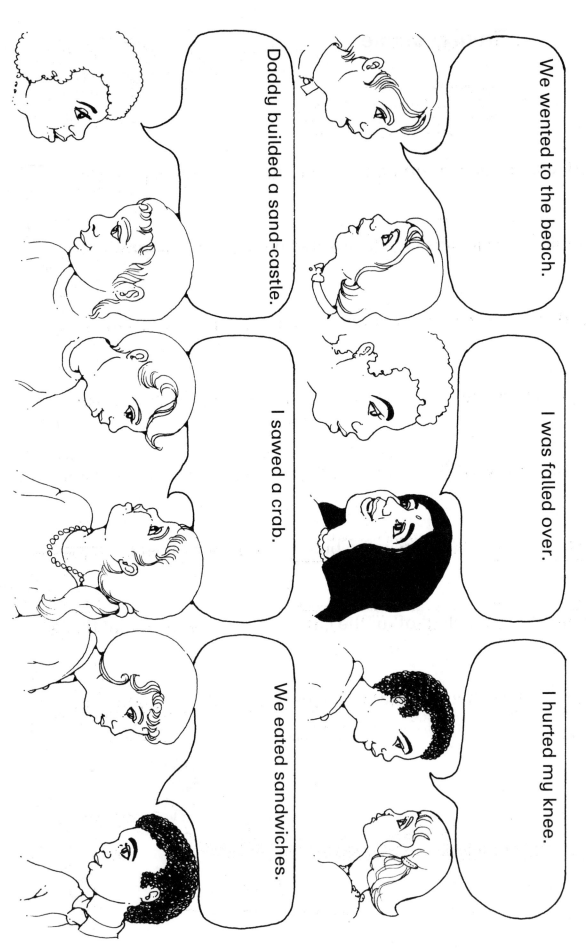

To be

1. We was late home last night.

2. You was not in the classroom.

3. They was fighting.

4. They is not coming with us.

5. They does not have to look at the book.

6. They has all got it wrong.

7. I is feeling ill.

8. I does not like fish.

9. I has got spots all over me.

10. We is running in a race.

11. I is not going to do it.

Stop, thief!

The sly old fox creeps along the wall. He drops down into the back garden and runs up to the kitchen window. Mrs Widder puts the cake on the window-sill to cool. She whistles to herself. The fox jumps up and grabs the cake. Mrs Widder does not hear anything. The fox leaps down and runs across the garden. Back in the den the vixen feeds her cubs on the delicious Christmas cake.

Name _____

Feeding time at the zoo

The camels was thirsty.

The elephants has all been fed bananas.

The rhino get the leaves by mistake.

The penguins is having fresh fish.

The hippo do like to have his back scratched.

The parrots is fond of nuts.

For the humming-birds a tune were not enough.

The vultures is very happy to eat meat.

The keeper go round the zoo with a smile for every animal.

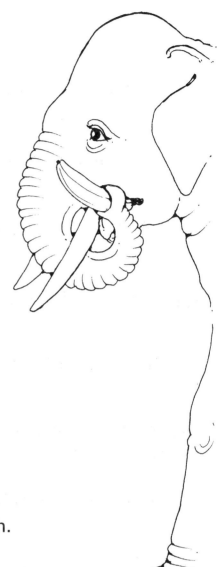

Copymaster 34

Name it!

We lioned down the street elephanting and pigging. The gang of

boys giraffed after us. We owled a few seconds start and pigeoned

for the park. We hippoed into a clump of bushes. My heart vultured

loudly and I turtled not to monkey. The gang of boys lioned into the

park and began to ostrich for us. They heroned into bushes and

eagled up trees. In the end they got kittened and went to trout about

on the swings. After a while they dolphined off, parroting and

stoating. Jane and I hedgehogged out from our hiding place. Our

clothes were tortoised. Mum would be tiggered with us.

Nonsense verbs

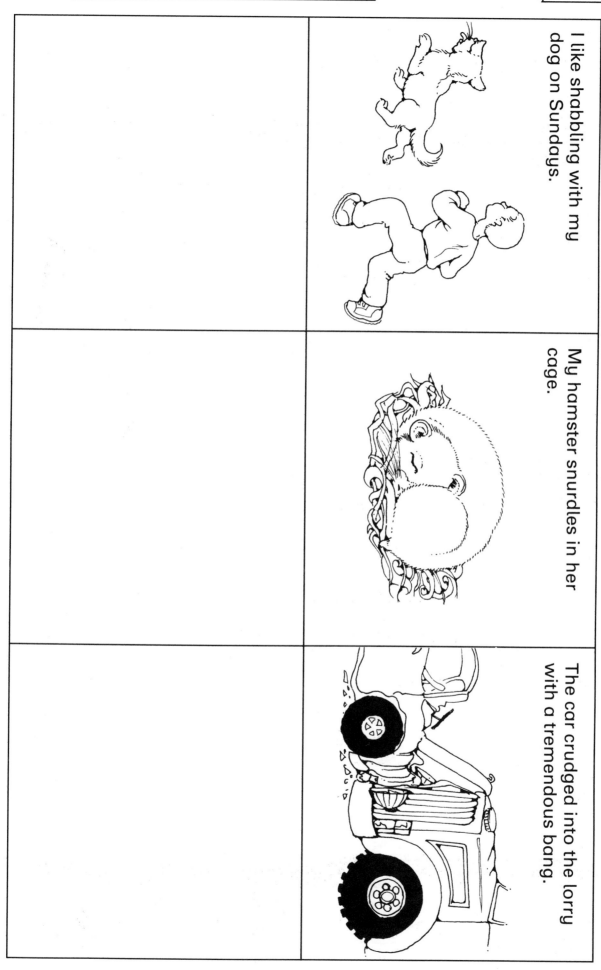

I like shabbling with my dog on Sundays.

My hamster snurdles in her cage.

The car crudged into the lorry with a tremendous bang.

Stormy night

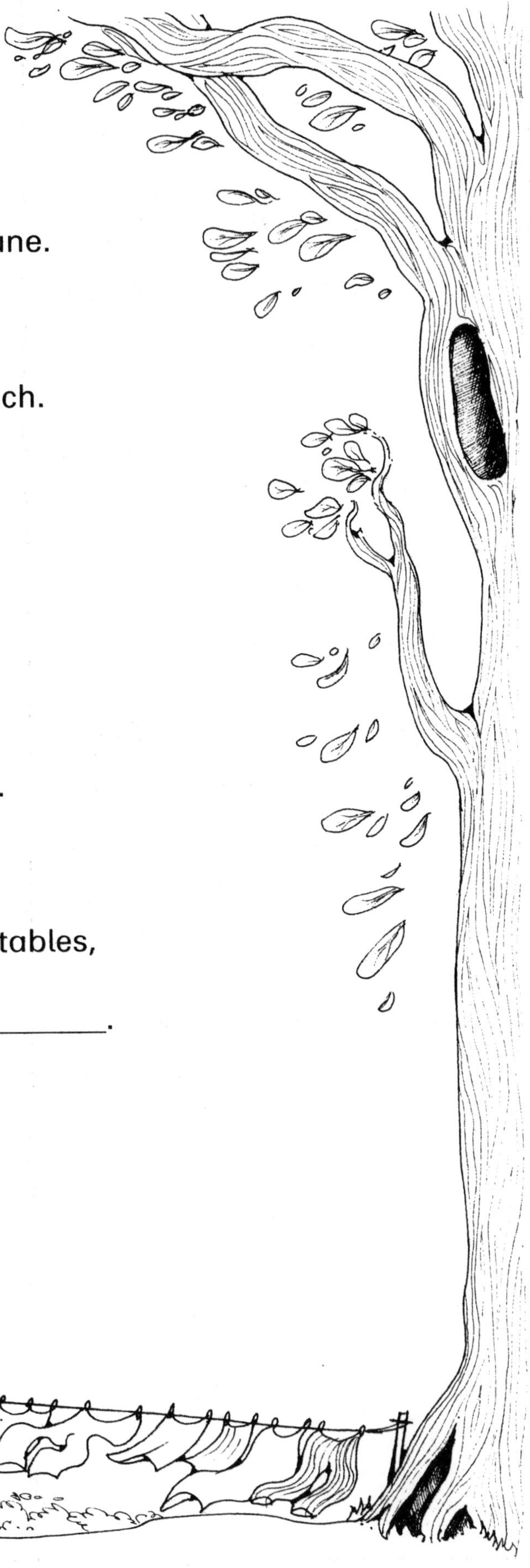

The thunder _____

as it _____ down Lynsted Lane.

The trees _____.

Leaves _____ on every branch.

The wind _____

the rooks from their nests.

Tiles _____.

Clothes on the washing-line

_____ across back gardens.

The streets _____,

cats _____ beneath kitchen tables,

dogs _____, babies _____.

Lightning _____.

The storm _____.

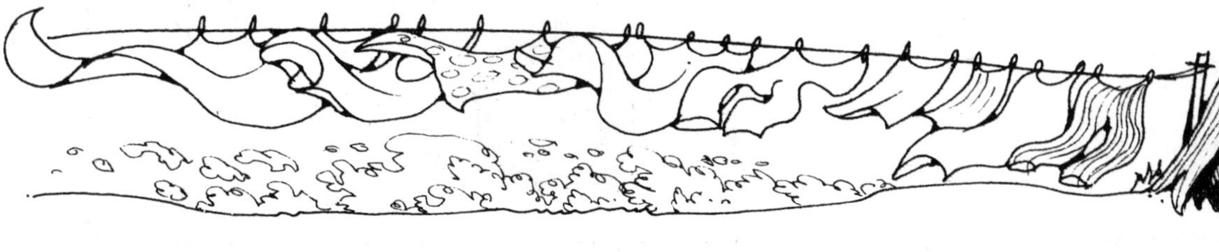

The great adverb hunt

Lazy adverbs

Slowly, the bus crawls through the traffic,
silently, the raindrop slips down the window,
slowly, the snail creeps along the branch,
silently, memories murmur in my mind,
slowly, the dust settles on to my palm,
silently, the sunlight brushes your hair,
slowly, the tree grows high above the house,
silently, the moon stares down at me,
slowly, time draws us on to its end.

Nice one!

She came into the room **nicely** and everyone clapped **nicely**.

The hawk hovered **nicely** and swooped **nicely**.

The mouse scurried **nicely** for safety.

The guns fired **nicely** and the sound echoed.

She answered **nicely** and the Doctor laughed **nicely**.

He stroked the horse **nicely**.

They sat down **nicely** and waited **nicely**.

He waited **nicely** lying on the river-bank.

She fell down **nicely** and hurt herself.

Jupiter snarled **nicely** and we ran away **nicely**.

Building a glider

Jane picked up the wings _____ly. _____ly she

pushed them into place. _____ly she squeezed glue on to the

surface. She waited _____ly as the glue set. _____ly

she launched the plane. The plane seemed to float _____ly and

_____ly. Jane laughed _____ly as the plane glided

_____ly. She had made it by herself, and now she looked on

_____ly. At last the glider drifted down landing

_____ly. Jane _____ly lifted it up. It was

_____ly the best she had ever made.

Because

I like sausages because they sizzle,

I do not like cats because they scratch,

I like _____ because

_____,

I do not like _____ because

_____,

Secrets

It's a secret

but I saw Superman eating lunch.

It's a secret

but I saw an octopus dancing the tango.

It's a secret

but my dog can sing.

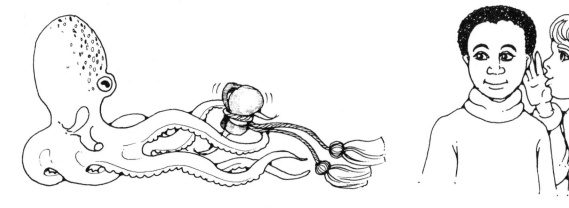

A good excuse?

Five good reasons why I am late for school this morning.

1. I would have been early but

2. I was on my way when

3. I was walking down the road and

4. I was late because

5. I was hurrying but

Five good reasons why I have not done my homework.

1. I started and

2. I got home early but

3. I was working hard until

4. I finished my work but

5. I did the work and then

Copymaster 44

A bad day

I woke early _____ missed the postman. I went

downstairs _____ had breakfast. I did not know

_____ I would get to school on time. The bus came

early _____ I was soon standing in the playground

on my own! I like being at school early _____ the

first person in school is allowed to feed the rabbits. I gave

them water _____ plenty of straw. I wanted to ask

the teacher _____ I could clean them out

_____ I went to the staff room. Miss Moynihan said

that I could clean them out _____ it was playtime.

_____ the first lesson we had P.E. _____ I

couldn't do any _____ I had forgotten my kit. I

wanted to join in _____ it was impossible! Miss

Moynihan never lets us do P.E. _____ we do not have

the right clothes.

but and either neither nor after later so however but
because then if as for yet when though unless since while

Name _____

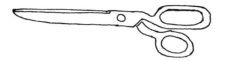

Conjunctions

Once upon a time there was a giant and he lived in a cave and he was

a very fierce giant and he frightened everyone who lived near and he

used to wait by the stream for the children then he would grab them

and pop them into his sack then he would carry them back to his cave.

One morning Sandy got caught and the giant stuffed her into his bag

and she wondered how she would escape and then he began to walk up

the mountain and he was going to cook her and then she found a pair of

scissors in her pocket then she cut open the sack and jumped out then

she put some rocks in the sack then when the giant got to the cave he

tipped the rocks out and then he roared with anger.

Spot the duck

behind in under beside up between against below by with beneath down near on off opposite

above   across   against   along   behind
below   beneath   between   beside   by   down
in   near   on   opposite   over   through
towards   under   up   upon

Where is the cat?

Name _____

Position poem

Aboard the raft the sailors lay,
across the seas the islands waited,
on the horizon the sun sat,
behind the clouds the universe watched,
below the waves the sharks circled,
between the hours the sailors prayed,
beyond the horizon a ship sailed,
on the waves white foam danced,
within an hour hope would arrive.

Pronouns

Tommy Brown asked Tommy Brown's Mum if Tommy Brown could

use Tommy Brown's bike. Mrs Brown said that Tommy Brown could

use Tommy Brown's bike as long as Tommy Brown was careful

with Tommy Brown's bike and that Tommy Brown should be back

home by tea-time or Tommy Brown's Mum would be cross.

"Are _____ sure that is _____?" _____ asked.

"_____ is mine," _____ replied. "And _____

am not going to give _____ to them, if that is what

_____ are thinking." "But _____ is ours," _____

shouted. "Well," said the teacher, "I don't know if _____ is

_____ or _____ but for the time being _____

will be mine. _____ is time _____ stopped arguing

and began to learn to share!"

you   we   he   she   they   it   me   us   him   her   them   it   yours

Copymaster 50

Whose skates?

Zandra and I are off to the ice-rink. We have new skates. Tony and Trina

have old skates. We must be careful not to muddle _____ with

_____. _____ are the red ones with silver glitter on

them. _____ are the ones with blue strips.

"Look over there, I can see Tony and Trina. Have they got

_____ skates? Oh yes, they have _____ and these are

_____ and these are _____."

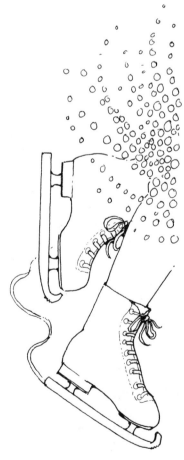

mine   yours   ours   its   his   hers   theirs   their

Escape!

Catch _____ antelope

Catch _____ aardvark

Catch _____ ant-eater

Catch _____ adder

Catch _____ emu

Catch _____ impala

Catch _____ iguana

Catch _____ ostrich

Catch _____ orangutang

Name _____

Cut-up sentences

Noun	Verb	Preposition	Noun
The builder	walked	to	the flats.
The dog	growled	at	the kitten.
The lorry	stopped	at	the lights.
The dolphin	swam	in	the sea.
The hippo	lay	in	the sun.
The children	danced	in	the gym.

Spot the word

The funfair glittered. Simon could see the bright lights flash and could

hear the sound of the organ spilling out its tune into the frosty, dark

night. He walked as quickly as he could down Bridge Street and ran

across the park. He could see Sam waiting for him by the hot dog

stall. Sam was halfway through a hot dog, his lips smeared with a

streak of red.

They took their first ride on the dodgems. The tiny cars were like fat

beetles bumping and crashing into each other. Sam's blond hair

flew back and his eyes seemed to stand out as he screeched round

the track. Two girls were watching them and giggling. They were

sharing a large stick of pink candy floss. It was Josie and Sharma.

Simon wondered whether Kay would be with them.

Name _____

Adjective								
Noun								
Verb								
Preposition								
Noun								

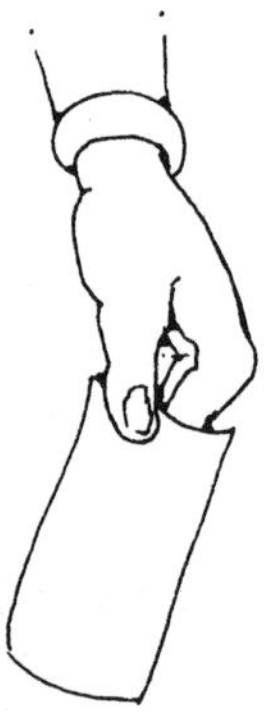

Consequences

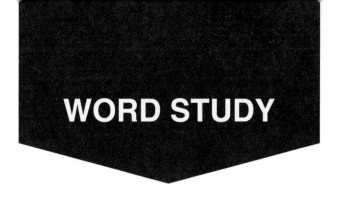

WORD STUDY

This section comprises a series of games, interactive texts and activities which aim to develop an interest in words and an understanding of the patterns of language. Many of the activities build upon a child's natural desire to invent and play, through which language can be explored and savoured.

The copymasters will enable teachers to discuss the use of words with the children, developing their awareness of vocabulary and its possibilities. There will be opportunities for their vocabulary to be: 'extended through consideration and discussion of words with similar meanings, opposite meanings, and words with more than one meaning.' (English in the National Curriculum, May 1994.) The activities will often require the children to use dictionaries; a valuable skill.

Copymaster 56 (Babies)
This is a simple game where the children match the adults to the respective juveniles. Ask the children to write a series of sentences that include the names of the 'babies'.

Copymaster 57 (Whose home?)
Ask the children to match the creatures to their respective homes. They should then select certain creatures and write a sentence about each in the space provided. The teacher could invite the children to write down a fact or a question for each of their selected creatures.

Copymaster 58 (Computers rhyme?)
The children complete the poem by filling in the gaps with appropriate rhyming words. They could begin by thinking of pairs or groups of rhyming words and listing them. For example: big, fig, wig, rig, dig. As the children progress, suggest that they use a couplet format such as:

You make me feel like a pound of jelly,
you make me feel like Big Daddy's belly.

Copymaster 59 (Swap a sound)
In this poem the rhymes have been swapped around. Challenge the children to make the poem rhyme again. For instance, the opening couplet could read: 'The brown bear drones, the lonely wolf moans'. The children could cross out and rewrite parts of the text. When the poems are complete, they should be read aloud and compared. Some of the verb endings will have to be altered according to whether the nouns are singular or plural.

Copymaster 60 (Smiling similes)
Encourage the children to think of commonly used similes, such as: as white as snow, as black as night.

Then ask them to create totally new similes to write on the copymaster. Here are some examples which can be used as prompts: as quick as a smack, as dark as a drain, as cool as lemonade, as sharp as a nettle sting.

Copymaster 61 (Over the top)
The children should complete the first set of similes so that they are exaggerations. For instance, 'as quick as a cheetah with jet-powered paws'. The secret is to add an extra dimension. An example of a 'humble simile' could be, 'as slow as a tortoise with brakes on'.

Copymaster 62 (Antonyms)
Explain that words that have opposite meanings are called antonyms. The children should circle and match the opposites. Encourage them to generate their own collection of antonyms.

Copymaster 63 (Animal idioms)
An idiom is a saying in which words have a different meaning to what seems to be the case. For example, 'to lose your head' is an idiom – it doesn't literally mean your head has dropped off! Ask the children to add to this collection of idioms. They could then be used as a source for story writing; the children select an idiom and write the story of how the saying came into being.

Copymaster 64 (Odd idioms)
This copymaster demonstrates how to twist idioms round, taking their meanings literally. The children could try doing the same using the list supplied, supplemented by any others they can think of. The teacher may need to provide the children with a number of examples before they begin.

Copymaster 65 (Things they say to me)
This activity is intended to encourage the children to listen critically to what others are saying. Ask them to collect a list of sayings by listening to their teachers and people at home. When they have made a collection, ask them to write their own poem. Read aloud this example:

I hate it when they say:
When you have quite finished,
Are you listening?
We'll see,
When you lot have simmered down,
Are those hands supposed to be clean?
You don't do that at home so don't do it here,
When I have everybody's attention,
That bed is not made,
Wait until your Dad gets home,
We will go when everyone is quiet,
Don't you dare…

Copymaster 66 (Alliteration)
Alliteration is a sound effect in a sentence, created when several words close together begin with the same sound or letter/s. The children should create their own alliterative sentences for members of their class. Afterwards, they could illustrate each sentence.

Copymaster 67 (Choose again)
This copymaster is in two sections. In the first section there is a long list of words. Ask the children to select three coloured crayons, and use one colour to underline or circle words that mean the same as **look**, another colour for words that mean the same as **said** and another colour for words that mean the same as **move**. In the second section there are three columns for the children to list further alternatives to these three commonly used words. The children could cut out the lists and paste them into their word books.

Copymaster 68 (Hidden words)
This is a useful time filler. The children should see how many words they can create from the large words provided. For example, a, as, an, ant, at, sat, son and sun, could be created from the word astronaut.

Copymaster 69 (The hundred letter name)
This is the name of a girl from Honolulu, registered in 1967. It means, 'the fragrant, abundant, beautiful blossoms begin to fill the air of the hills and valleys throughout the length and breadth of these wonderful islands at daybreak'. The idea is to see how many words can be made out of this name, but the children can only use the letters which appear once. Therefore, they will need to strike off letters as they are used.

This lengthy name might begin an investigation into long names, long words, short names and words, long place names and unusual names. *The Guinness Book of Records* is a useful reference source.

Copymaster 70 (Word strings)
Challenge the children to make as long a word string as they can. Each word should begin with the last letter of the previous word. Some children could just try one category, either 1. animals, 2. places, 3. names or 4. actions. The first word string could be ca**t** – **t**ige**r** – **r**at – **t**errapi**n** – **n**ew**t** – **t**urtl**e** – **e**lephant. Some children may need to be supplied with dictionaries.

Copymaster 71 (Acrostic speed game)
This could be a timed activity. The children should write a word beginning with each letter which is associated with the creature. For example:

Dirty
Overweight
Growling

Provide the children with dictionaries for this activity.

Copymaster 72 (Initials)
First the children identify the initials of their first names and surnames. They should then answer the questions using two words that begin with these initials. As my name is Pie Corbett, I would answer as follows: What is your favourite food? **P**ink **C**abbage. What do you like doing most at home? **P**icking **C**arrots. Some replies could be more bizarre: What do you like reading about? **P**retty **C**ornflakes. A dictionary is essential for this game. Extend the activity by asking the children to invent questions for each other.

Copymaster 73 (English?)
Can the children guess which countries these words come from? After they have guessed, they should look them up in a good dictionary. This activity should be accompanied by a discussion about how language is shaped by the influence of others – conquering forces as well as cultural ones! The children could then make collections of 'new words' (less than ten years old) or local words, computer words, American football terms or family words.

Copymaster 74 (Making words)
The children should join the parts of words from the two columns to invent new words. Other letters could be added if needed. Ask them to use these new words – or borrow their friends' – to write sentences or a newspaper story, letter or diary entry. The final draft of their work can be written in the space provided.

Copymaster 75 (Silly sentences)
Homonyms are words that are spelled the same but have two or more meanings. The children should write a series of sentences using the homonyms listed at the bottom of the page. They may need to be prompted with another example as well as the one provided on the copymaster: I gave a wave as I swam in the waves.

Copymaster 76 (Homophones)
Homophones are words that sound the same but are spelled differently and have different meanings. The copymaster provides the children with a collection of pairs of homophones which they could add to. They should write sentences that use both words at once. For example: I saw a **bare bear bare** its teeth, or I went **pale** as I picked up the **pail** of milk.

Copymaster 77 (A fairy tale)
The passage is full of homophones. The children should proofread it and change the spellings as necessary. Encourage them to use a dictionary to check the meanings of these words.

Copymaster 78 (Synonyms)
Explain ·that synonyms are words which have similar meanings. The children should provide synonyms for the highlighted words. Emphasise that the alternative words should make the letter sound less pompous and more exciting. The children may need to use a dictionary for this activity.

Copymaster 79 (Eastern sayings)
Ask the children to provide their own definitions for these sayings. These could be brainstormed in groups and noted at the bottom of the copymaster. They could

then select one of the sayings and write a story about how it came into being. Alternatively, they might like to relate their story orally.

Copymaster 80 (New proverbs)
This is a list of traditional proverbs. A proverb is a wise saying that has been in existence for many years. The children should create new proverbs from these old ones – an example is provided. They could then collect more proverbs by asking people at home. Here are some examples which could be used as prompts:

Look before you leap – *Look before you cross the road*

Too many cooks spoil the broth – *Too many cats will fight over the cream*

Leave well alone – *Leave sleeping snakes alone or they bite*

An apple a day keeps the doctor away – *An onion a day keeps everyone away!*

Don't put all your eggs into one basket – *Don't put two cats into a basket or they'll fight.*

Babies

eagle	cub
eel	piglet
chicken	tadpole
owl	lamb
human	calf
fox	pup
dog	cub
duck	eaglet
cow	elver
sheep	chick
goose	toddler
frog	duckling
pig	puppy
lion	gosling
seal	owlet

Whose home?

Animals		Homes	
mouse	sparrow	nest	cave
pig	dog	kennel	hive
rabbit	horse	burrow	shed
snail	bear	shell	stable
spider	bee	web	hole
squirrel	cow	drey	sty

Computers rhyme?

They have programmed me to rhyme

and I do it all the time.

I rhyme goody with woody,

zany with brainy,

car with _____,

stay with _____,

rare with _____,

sack with _____,

dry with _____,

claw with _____,

flow with _____,

plough with _____,

chip with _____,

prop with _____,

scrape with _____,

flan with _____,

mad with _____,

grip with _____,

fate with _____.

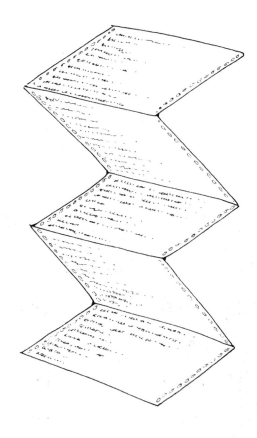

Swap a sound

The brown bear sings,
the lonely wolf speaks,

the busy bees joke,
the dying men prays,

the sad priest drones,
the donkey rings,

Tom cracks a moan,
frogs jump and patter,

raindrops howl,
pots and pans croak,

the telephone brays,
the choir boy growls,

the whistle clatters,
nobody shrieks.

Name _____

Smiling similes

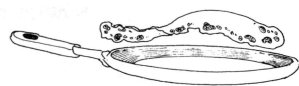

as quick as

as small as

as funny as

as dry as

as dull as

as deep as

as hot as

as cold as

as slippery as

as hungry as

as red as

as blue as

as sharp as

as quiet as

as loud as

as still as

as sweet as

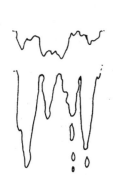

Copymaster 60

Over the top

The boastful simile

I was as cool as

as quick as

as brilliant as

as tall as

as sharp as

as happy as

as useful as

and as popular as

The humble simile

I was as slow as

as shy as

as fat as

as ugly as

as daft as

as dull as

as dreary as

and as helpless as

Copymaster 61

Name _____

Antonyms

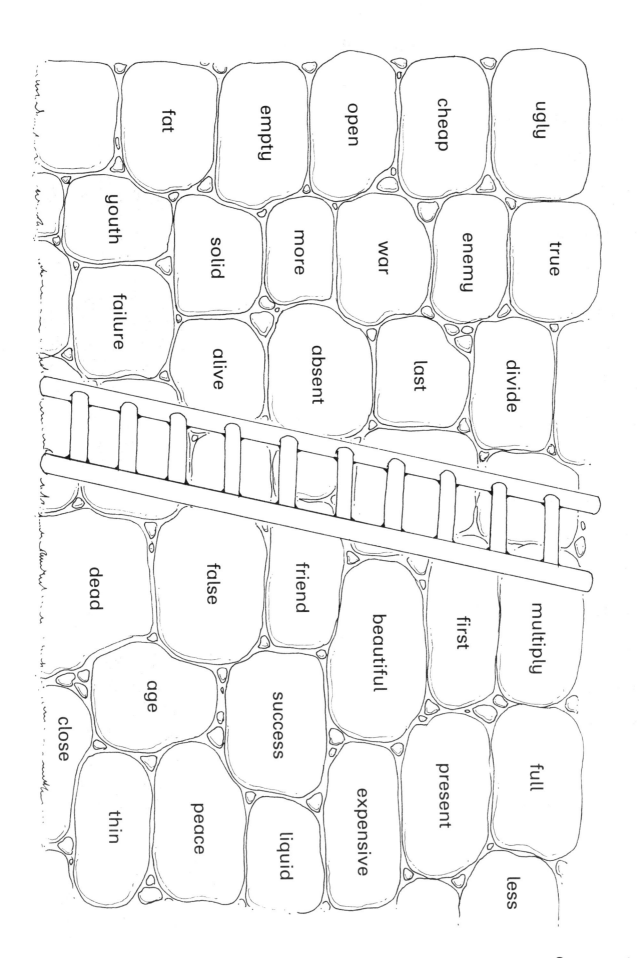

fat
empty
open
cheap
ugly

youth
solid
more
war
enemy
true

failure
alive
absent
last
divide

dead
false
friend
beautiful
first
multiply

close
age
success
expensive
present
full

thin
peace
liquid
less

Animal idioms

to have ants in your pants

to have a bee in your bonnet

to have a frog in your throat

to take the bull by the horns

to look a gift horse in the mouth

to smell a rat

to bark up the wrong tree

to be a cold fish

to let the cat out of the bag

to be a wolf in sheep's clothing

Odd idioms

1. Sally said that we should
   keep our eyes peeled. We tried
   but it hurt too much.

2. I hit the nail on the head.
   It screamed with pain.

3. My teacher went bananas.
   She turned bright yellow.

4. I had my head in the clouds.
   The thunder gave me a
   headache.

laughed her head off   in hot water   lend me your ears   get cold feet

have an ear to the ground   on its last legs   in the dog house

long in the tooth   it's raining cats and dogs   missed the boat

cat got your tongue   bottle up your feelings   no leg to stand on

Things they say to me

I hate it when they say:

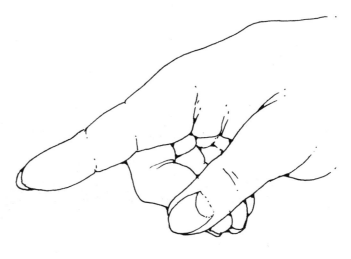

Alliteration

Paula picked a piece of pink pineapple patiently.

Tommy tickled two tiny toes.

Sandy smiled savagely at Cindy's silly saucepan.

Barry bravely built a big bridge.

Choose again

wave   creep   complained   dance   flee   hissed   whispered

pace   yelled   stare   strike   bounded   ride   mouthed

glare   shouted   tiptoe   gaze   see   walk   tread

crawled   glance

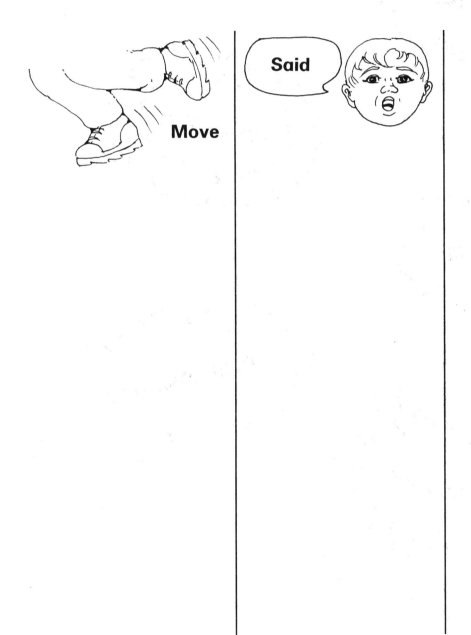

Move

Said

Look

Hidden words

ASTRONAUT

ANTEDILUVIAN

SYMPATHIZE

EXCLAMATIONS

CONGLOMERATE

SUBTERRANEAN

The hundred letter name

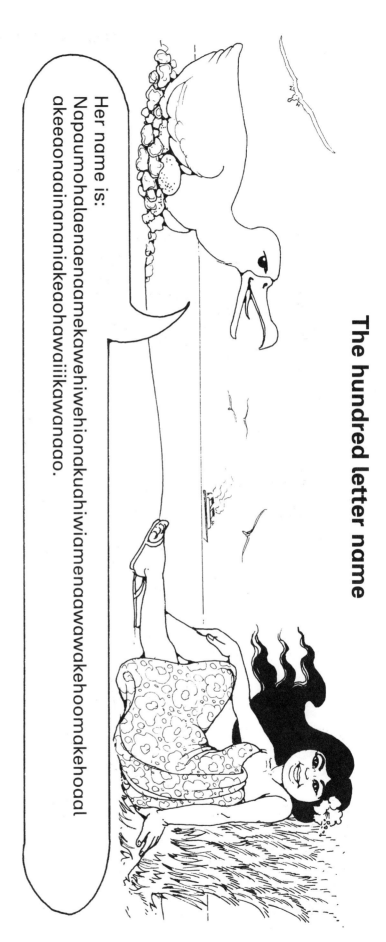

Her name is:
Napaumohalaenaenaamekawehiwehionakuahiwiamenaawawawakehoomakehoaakeeaonaainananiakeaohawaiiikawanaao.

Word strings

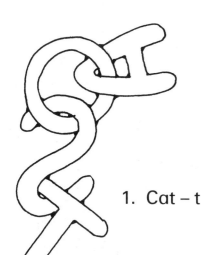

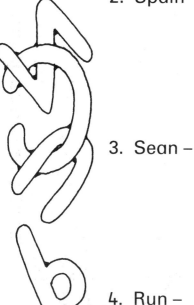

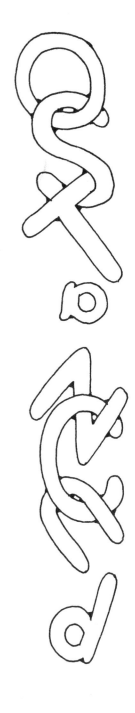
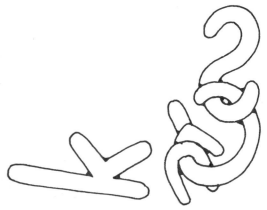

1. Cat – t

2. Spain –

3. Sean –

4. Run –

Acrostic speed game

D   C

O   A

G   T

A   H

N   E

T   N

B   C

E   O

E   W

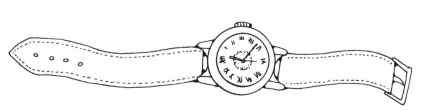

Copymaster 71

Initials

Name: Initials:

What is your favourite food?

What do you like doing most at home?

Which is your favourite lesson?

What would you like to do when you leave school?

What do you like writing about?

What is your favourite television programme?

What do you think the Prime Minister eats for breakfast?

What should your teacher do on Saturday?

English?

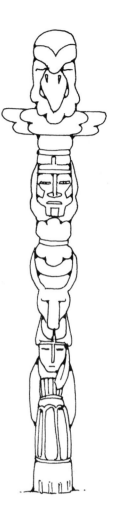

cafe	leg
cul-de-sac	mutton
duvet	pork
totem	bungalow
tomato	juggernaut
loch	algebra
pyjamas	sugar
wood	prairie

XY_2

YX_2

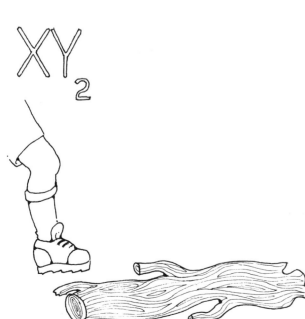

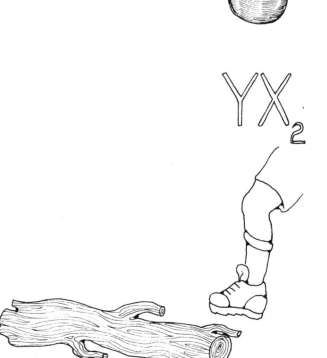

Making words

Fri	ment
Cr	stly
Spl	eavy
Tr	usk
Sh	iable
Th	atch
Pl	ory
Tr	ouse
Cl	ess
Con	eer
Hun	oast
Tim	in
Reg	ibbing

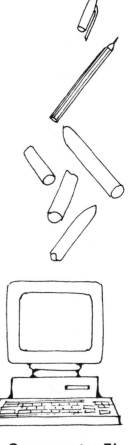

Copymaster 74

Silly sentences

Watch out, I am going to **watch** my **watch**.

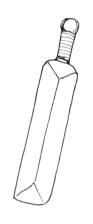

wave   sink   trip   arm   match   jam   bat   fan   rock   back   light

Homophones

bare	bear		knows	nose
blew	blue		leak	leek
bean	been		meat	meet
flour	flower		main	mane
hair	hare		pail	pale
road	rowed		their	there
heard	herd		pear	pair
ball	bawl		pause	paws
hole	whole		piece	peace
knew	new		reed	read

A fairy tale

The king's sun stared at the princess who was bound to the steak. The son blazed down and he knew that their was no thyme to waist. He wood have to hope and prey that his plan wood work. He pealed off a strip of the ship's sale and rapped it round his waste. There was no thyme to practise. He through himself into the see to dampen his clothes. "Now," shouted the princess. He through himself write into the read flames that flickered at her feat. His steal knife cut her bonds. "You are a brave sole," she said.

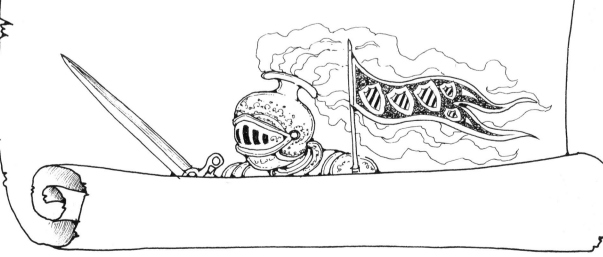

Synonyms

Piper's Cottage,

Piglin Bland

Baconshire.

3rd May 1820.

Dear Tom,

I was sorry to have **departed** so soon from your **nice**

accommodation. I savoured my **annual trek**, and the **lovely**

banquet that we **enjoyed** with your friends was

marvellous. I could not **conceal** my pleasure when I **looked**

up at your big apple trees covered in such **big**, red fruit.

I came back home on the train. When I **got** home there

was a light on and it looked as if there had been a

burglary! I **came** up the path and **looked** through the

window. There was **ancient** Mr Foxglove and **avaricious**

Mr Stoatly **talking** and **laughing** as they **consumed** my

home-made wine. They **got** quite a shock when I **came** in!

You should have seen them **run** down the path!

Best wishes,

Your friend Freddy.

Name _____

Eastern sayings

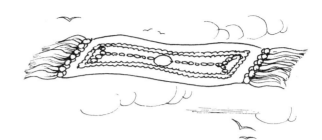

The idiot's meal is safe inside the clever man's stomach.

The thunder-cloud does not always bring rain.

Snakes shed their skins but will still sting.

Rumour has quick feet.

The earth can feed man's need but not his greed.

The mouse is small through fear of the cat.

The poor man wants only bread, the rich man

wants the world.

Copymaster 79

New proverbs

No smoke without fire ———► *No pain without a pinch*

A fool and his money are soon parted

An apple a day keeps the doctor away

Birds of a feather flock together

The early bird catches the worm

Don't count your chickens till they're hatched

Look before you leap

When the cat is away the mice will play

Two heads are better than one

Out of the frying pan, into the fire

New brooms sweep clean

Too many cooks spoil the broth

Great minds think alike

Don't put all your eggs into one basket

No news is good news

Let sleeping dogs lie

Leave well alone

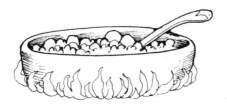

SENTENCES

This section aims to raise the children's awareness of what makes sentences work. It provides opportunities for critical reflection on the effective use of vocabulary and the on-going development of terminology. The children should learn to recognise effective writing, through redrafting, proofreading and responding to written texts. Emphasis is also placed upon developing a sense of the respective positions of different types of words within sentences. One approach is to confront incorrect or poorly constructed sentences by first discussing faults and then amending them.

The section ends by considering the demands upon language when writing for different audiences. Pupils are encouraged to read as a writer, and respond to written texts by highlighting effective uses of language.

Copymaster 81 (Extending sentences)

This copymaster focuses upon the basic components of a sentence. The children should complete the sentences as imaginatively as possible. Remind them that each sentence should make sense, contain a verb, start with a capital letter and end with a full stop, question mark or exclamation mark.

Copymaster 82 (Sentence scraps)

The 'scraps' should be cut out and new sentences created (with capital letters and full stops). The children may need some extra words to make the task easier. The new sentences may be written out and then read aloud for full effect. Which types of words are essential? Can the scraps be categorised in any way? Which are good for starting or ending sentences or for the action?

Copymaster 83 (Number plate sentences)

In the first column, the children collect letters from number plates. They should then invent simple sentences using these letters. For example:

JOG **J**ohn **o**rganises **g**racefully.
MNJ **M**elanie **n**ever **j**umps.
EGL **E**ddie **g**ently **l**aughed.

Copymaster 84 (Cocktail sentences)

Challenge the children to make up as many sentences as they can using the words listed. Each sentence should contain a noun, adjective and verb. These could be written in the space provided. Unusual and memorable combinations of words should be encouraged. Ask the children to write sentences without using words from the verb column. Is this possible?

Copymaster 85 (The word waiter)

I often use a 'word waiter' when I visit schools to run writers' workshops. The children should use all the words (adding different endings or prefixes if necessary) 'served up' in a story, diary entry, letter, newspaper item or poem. The story could be a short story, a descriptive passage or a mini-saga of no more than 150 words. There is space for the children's final draft of their chosen piece of writing on the copymaster. It may be appropriate to read aloud the examples given below, although they could stifle individuality.

100 word mini-saga

It was night-time. Outside the wind was blowing a gale and branches were banging against the window. Simon thought that he heard a key turn in the lock. He went down the stairs and saw a thin shadow on the wall. It had to be a burglar. Simon did not know what to do. He threw a mirror at the wall and it broke into a thousand, glistening splinters. When he looked again the shadow was still there. He picked up an umbrella and charged. There was a squeal from under his feet. It wasn't a burglar. It was a cat.

Newspaper item

Last night there was a Christmas concert held at the Broad Stairs Primary School. The school had been decorated with thin home-made stained-glass windows. The children performed a play called 'The Cat's Magic Mirror'. Jessica Eddershort had a major part in the play. She was an angel dressed in a glistening white costume. Because of the bad weather there was a small audience. However, the headteacher said: "The key to a good performance is plenty of practice."

Poem

Stars glisten.
The night creeps upstairs
like a cat.
The thin moon,
like a slice of a mirror
is hidden by clouds.
Curtains scrape
at the window panes.
Downstairs,
a key turns in the lock.
The house closes
its tired eyes.

Copymaster 86 (Muddled sentences)
All the words in these sentences have been muddled up. The children should rewrite them correctly. Suggest they read their versions aloud to a partner to see if they 'sound right'.

Copymaster 87 (Happy holiday?)
The children should read the passage through and then reorganise the words in the sentences so that it makes sense.

Copymaster 88 (Spot the sentence)
The children should tick the appropriate boxes to indicate whether these are sentences or not. Reading each sentence aloud will help the children to assess whether it 'sounds' as if something is missing. Where the sentences are incomplete or do not make sense, the children could rewrite them.

Copymaster 89 (Postcards)
Ask the children to imagine that they are holidaying in the places listed on the copymaster. Challenge them to compose a postcard to send to their friends from each destination. Each sentence should begin with a letter from the name of the country, as shown in the example. Emphasise that they should write in complete sentences.

Copymaster 90 (The wish)
This copymaster involves a cloze procedure, where more and more of the words have been taken away. The children should rewrite and complete the passage, building up a sensible story. They should add as many words as they require, not necessarily the number which appear to fit in the gaps. They should use the space provided on the copymaster for their final version.

Copymaster 91 (Fears)
On this copymaster the children should write the final version of a poem about their fears, using the repeating phrase 'I am afraid of' to link their ideas. Each time they write a sentence they must complete it with a full stop. To make the activity more challenging, I have collected a number of words at the bottom of the page. The children should try to use one of the words in each sentence. Read out the following example, and invent a few new lines with the class before they begin.

> I am afraid of
> branches that tap at my window.
> I am afraid of
> dogs that growl at me.
> I am afraid of
> stairs that creak at night.

Copymaster 92 (Capture!)
Encourage the children to complete the poem using sentences. They could invent magical or impossible endings. Read this example to prompt them:

> I want to capture the sound of
> the trees sneezing in winter.
> I want to capture the feel of
> my parents arguing and hide it away.

> I want to capture the smell of
> the first day of a holiday
> and wear it as a scent.
> I want to capture the sight of
> my brother blowing his own trumpet.
> I want to capture the taste of
> the day when peace is complete.
> I want to capture the moment when
> the frost packs its bag and heads for home.
> I want to capture the memory of
> my Gran's smiling face
> and keep it alive forever.
> I want to capture the silence when
> two blades of grass kneel down.
> I want to capture the feeling of
> anger and dip it in a pool of tears.

Copymaster 93 (It could have been)
Young children often say 'it could of been', which is grammatically incorrect. This poem encourages them to practise using the correct form of the phrase. Read this example to the class:

> Last night,
> I heard a sound.
> It could have been my brother snoring.
> It could have been the trees complaining.
> It could have been the police on patrol.
> It could have been the moon yawning.

The poem should end by stating what did make the noise, in this case, it was only the sound of the television mumbling downstairs.

Copymaster 94 (Animal language)
The children should use the words listed on the copymaster to write a short passage that will fit in the space provided. However, they must not use the words as nouns. For example, they could write, the men were **rabbitting** but I felt **sheepish**. **I snaked** my way through the **herd** and tried to **bully** my way into the garden. How many of the words are they able to use?

This activity could be used in conjunction with that shown on copymaster 35.

Copymaster 95 (Writing speech)
This copymaster will need to be read aloud and discussed. Point out that in informal situations many people talk in this way. However, in a formal situation or when writing in standard English this type of speech would not be acceptable. The children's task is to rewrite the sentences in an acceptable form.

Copymaster 96 (For sale)
The children need to invent three 'for sale' signs from the notes provided. They must remember to 'dress up the goods' in order to sell them. So, 'ten-years-old' might be interpreted as 'traditional model'. Some parts of the notes could be omitted if the children think they are unnecessary. In groups, they should read aloud their advertisements and select the most effective ones.

90

Copymaster 97 (Nursery rewrite)
The children should choose a nursery rhyme to write in the space at the top of the sheet. In the boxes they rewrite the rhyme as a newspaper article, a diary entry and a letter. The teacher may need to discuss the styles of writing which are appropriate to the different purposes before the children begin the activity. The final results should be compared and discussed.

Copymaster 98 (Stop press!)
This chatty diary entry should be rewritten as a newspaper item in the space provided. The only problem is that the editor (the teacher) will only allow the reporter (the child) to write 100 words. Therefore, he/she may need to focus upon just a few of the main events in the passage. He/she could circle or underline key facts before starting to write his/her news item, providing a structure for his/her creative writing.

Copymaster 99 (Rewrite)
This chatty letter should be re-worded as a formal letter of complaint to Dinglefords Head Office. The children could use the bottom half of the copymaster for their final version. Read the letters aloud. Discuss whether they have the formal and persuasive tone necessary for this type of writing.

Copymaster 100 (Fact file)
The children should simplify this passage for a younger audience – let us say 6-year-olds. They could start by underlining the key information in the text. They should then simplify the language and trim the content. Their final versions could be read aloud, and if possible trialled with a group of infants.

Copymaster 101 (Improve this!)
This passage could be improved by adding or altering adjectives, adverbs or verbs. This needs to be done selectively in order to give power to the writing. Final versions should be read aloud and compared to see which are the most effective, and why.

Copymaster 102 (Jimmy Crackcorn)
Use this poem to initiate a discussion. Ask the children to circle or underline words and phrases (parts of a sentence) that are effective. (They could underline adjectives in one colour and verbs in another.) What did they like about the poem? What didn't they like? Did they understand all of the poem? Can they identify any language patterns? What sort of person or creature is Jimmy Crackcorn? Ask them to draw him. They might invent their own mythical person or creature and use a similar approach to write a poem. For example:

Who is that Father,
Walking in the sunset?
Why it is Jenny Greenteeth,
Waiting at the edge of the still pool,
Staring up from the water's edge,
With a string of weeds about her white neck …

Extending sentences

I like fish and chips

On Friday night we went to my nan's house

''Get out of here

The cat sat

The dog barked

I saw a seagull

The car drove

We ran down the street

There is an old lady

Sentence scraps

the brown cow

and

chugged up

till it

the old car

ran

jumped

across the field

Janet

kissed

the hill

in the

Caroline

stroked

smacked

purred

night

her teddy bear

quietly

in the waves

Number plate sentences

Letters	Sentences
J R Q	John runs quickly.
B F W	Bats fly well.
C C M	Cats can meow.
C E F	Carrie eats fish.

Name _____

 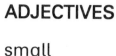

Cocktail sentences

ADJECTIVES	NOUNS	VERBS
small	grape	sing
smooth	gnat	giggle
rude	snail	whisper
fat	tortoise	fill
graceful	shoe	slice
strange	mirror	burn
sweet	tower	catch
sour	comic	forget

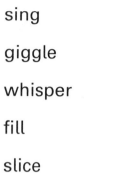

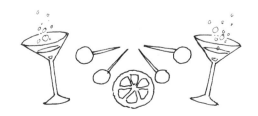

Copymaster 84

Name _____

The word waiter

night   glisten   key

cat   window   mirror   thin

stairs

Name _____

Muddled sentences

1. Fish and fingers like to eat Poppy Daisy.

2. Teddy plays in the ball with a garden.

3. The beach shines down on the sun.

4. Ice-creams lick if you do not melt them.

5. The bell scare a cat to wears the birds.

6. I am afraid of growl that dogs.

7. I go to sleep to want tonight.

8. Where is the butterflies about book?

9. When it will time be us for have to milk?

10. Australia has gone to year for a Tammy.

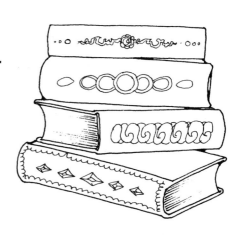

Copymaster 86

Happy holiday?

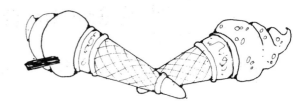

Last Dad was so burned that summer got hot top on. His patch bald
turned red quite. His peeled nose. So, made him Mum a hat wear.
Daft said he looked Dad hat up in a dressed. He hanky tried a but
that was good no. Afternoon one were we the beach on when Mum
cream some spread of right top on his head. He scalded like a
screamed cat. We laughed all him at. Don't I think thought he funny
very was it.

Name _____

Spot the sentence

Yes	No		
☐	☐	1.	Early in the morning a frog.
☐	☐	2.	From the top of the hill you could.
☐	☐	3.	After a silence, the rain began to fall.
☐	☐	4.	Rashid ran.
☐	☐	5.	Stop!
☐	☐	6.	Janet, a long time ago, gently.
☐	☐	7.	When it is dark.
☐	☐	8.	If it is your bat.
☐	☐	9.	Climb that gate, quick.
☐	☐	10.	In a few seconds.

 **Postcards**

I have been here for one week.

Today it is really sunny.

Angela has been eating the ice-creams.

Lee has gone for a swim in the sea.

Yours, with love, Betty.

I
N
D
I
A

A
F
R
I
C
A

A
M
E
R
I
C
A

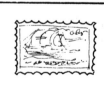

Copymaster 89

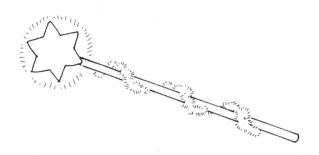

The wish

Once upon a time there was _____ small girl. She lived in

_____ tall block of flats. _____ lived alone with

_____ mother. The side they _____ on was always

just out _____ sun and all day _____ dark and

gloomy. It was one hundred _____ down to the _____,

and as her Mother had a bad _____ they hardly ever went

down. How the _____ wished she could play outside in

_____ . One day _____ . The little girl _____ .

It was extraordinary . She _____ . There _____ so

_____ and _____ .

Fears

I am afraid of ...

creak   dark   silent   monster   gloomy   bat   mirror   window

thunder   lightning   lonely   growl

Capture!

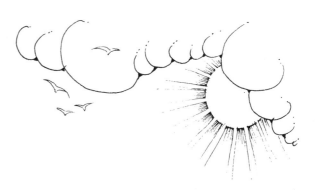

I want to capture the sound of

I want to capture the feel of

I want to capture the smell of

I want to capture the sight of

I want to capture the taste of

I want to capture the moment when

I want to capture the memory of

I want to capture the silence of

I want to capture the feeling of

It could have been

Last night,

I heard a sound.

It could have been

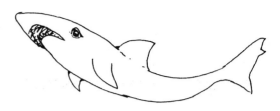

Animal language

rabbit   hare   lion   herd   beetle   sheepish   puffin   hounding

cheetah   snake   ewe   shark   pig   worm   bully   coward   horse

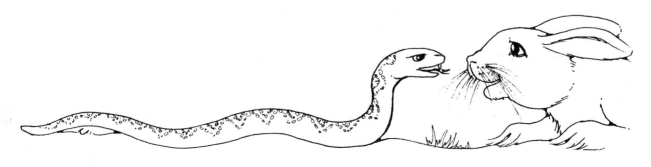

Copymaster 94

Writing speech

1. I've just done it, ain't I.

2. It makes sense, donnit?

3. Here, look at that one over there.

4. I ain't got none.

5. You lot, cut it out.

6. I've finished that an' all.

7. We was all there.

8. We don't talk about nothing.

9. I agree with yer, an all.

10. Have you seen my new bike what I got?

Copymaster 95

For sale

cat lovers only   lawn-mower   car   five kittens   £2   plenty of owners
eight-weeks-old   poor starter in cold weather   all black
10-year-old   purple and green   to be drowned if not sold   often breaks
down   rusted underneath   only good for   large boot   long grass
electric

Nursery rewrite

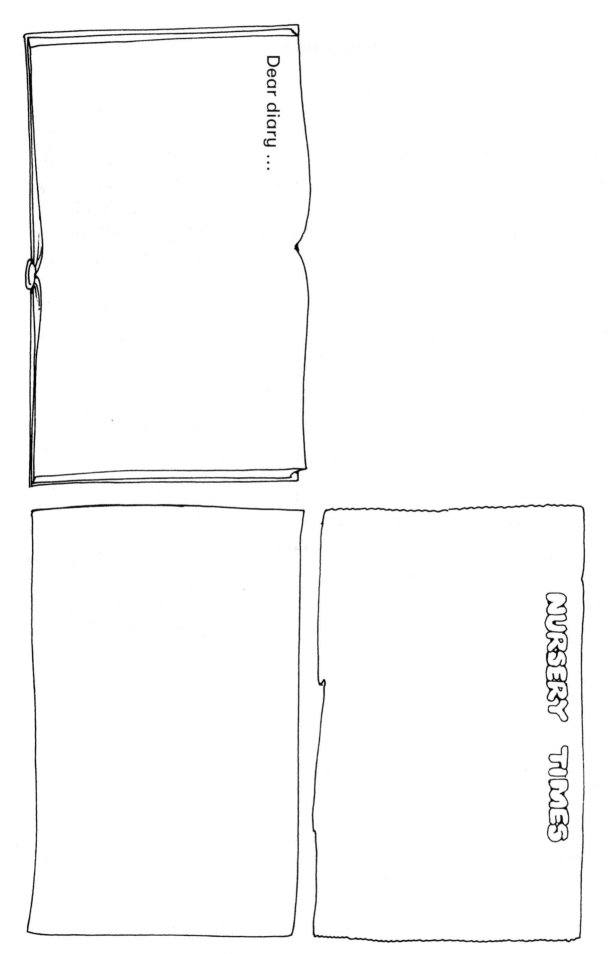

Dear diary …

NURSERY TIMES

Stop press!

Wednesday 24th January.

Well, what an exciting day. I was coming home down Bridge Street, when all of a sudden a man with a black mask on came shooting out of Huskins, the new toy shop down that road, and anyway this man shot out on to the street and a lady came after him shouting out stop thief. She was crying and when I got near her I saw it was Jane Silverbry who I used to be at school with. Just at that very moment a policeman came rushing down the street with an Alsatian on a lead and he let the Alsatian off the lead shouting – go on Prince – and the next thing you know – whammo! One thief caught! He had all the money from the till – Jane said it was over thirty pounds!

☆ STAR NEWS ☆

Rewrite

42 Grange Hights,
Oswald Road,
Tingletown,
Cudlingshire   G18 NM8.

1st April 2020.

Dear Sue,

I had a terrible time the other day. I went to the department store –
Dinglefords – to buy myself a video recorder. Well, I went in and
had a good look at all the things they had there. After a while this
young bloke came up to me and he wants to know what I'm doing
hanging around in the store! Can you believe it, he thinks that I've
nicked something. The next thing I know I've been taken into the
Manager's office and made to turn out my handbag. Well, as you
can imagine I had a few words to say to that young man, and I told
him that I would be writing to Head Office and I'd have a word or
two to say about him. I've been shopping in that store for twenty
years! Must go now, my Bill will be home soon.

Lots of kisses,

Josie.

Name _____

Fact file

| Keeping hermit crabs |

Hermit crabs can make interesting

and unusual pets, but they need proper

accommodation and a carefully balanced diet. It is

important to ensure that the crabs have a range of

different structures to climb, as in their natural environment they are

used to climbing trees. It is also important to provide them with plenty

of damp moss for burrowing, as in their natural habitat they like to hide

from predators. They should be fed a balanced diet of vegetables, fish

and fruit, and provided with a regular supply of freshwater.

Improve this!

One winter's evening we went for a walk across the fields. The snow fell.

We went across the fields, hands in our pockets. The wind was cold. I

had my scarf over my mouth. In the bottom field the sheep had come

together for warmth. My father and I took them towards the barn. We

counted them into the barn and found that one had gone. Somewhere

out in the darkness was a lost sheep. We went up and down the field. In

the end we came across it. The sheep was covered in snow. I got the

snow off its back and we tried to get the sheep to move, but it would not

move an inch. My father went off to get the tractor and a trailer and I

stayed with the sheep. It looked at me with its big eyes. I sat in the

darkness with the snow coming down talking to the sheep, until out of

the darkness came the tractor lights.

Jimmy Crackcorn

What is that
stalking through the dark
at the end of the road?

It's Jimmy Crackcorn, Mother.
Listen to him crack his knuckles
like dry bones breaking,
like gunshot on a still day,
like a whip's crack
on the slave's back.
Listen, Mother,
It's Jimmy Crackcorn.

Who is that
waiting at the edge of sleep
for the eyelids to slip shut
and the senses to drift away?

It's Jimmy Crackcorn, Mother.
Listen to him breathe
on to his cold hands.
His fingers are white
with the frost and the night.
Listen to the sudden rush of breath.
Listen to the last rasping cough of death.

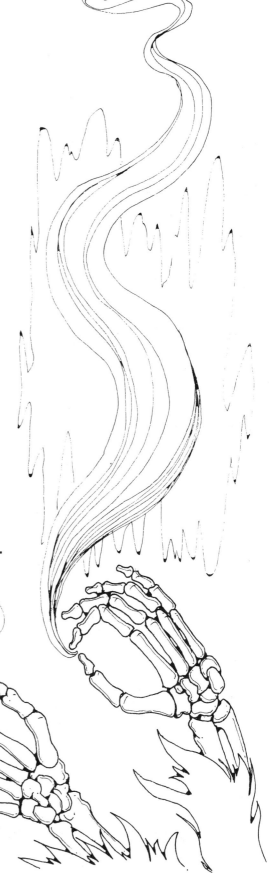

Copymaster 102

PUNCTUATION

This section focuses on the development of children's ability to use punctuation. The copymasters offer a range of activities to: introduce, practice and highlight different aspects of punctuation. They emphasise the need for punctuation – a convention that assists the reader. The gradual development of punctuation is also seen as a proofreading consideration. As children become more fluent in their writing, introduce punctuation through their reading and by demonstration. Discuss punctuation when you write in front of the children.

Much of this work will be targeted at groups of children, to be reinforced individually and occasionally through whole-class discussion and demonstration. Through using, creating and responding to different types of sentence and conventions, it is hoped that the children will develop a deeper understanding of this important area of English.

Copymaster 103 (Full stops)
Initially, this copymaster should be given to the children to read aloud. They will find this difficult to do. Point out that to make the text easier to read we need to help the reader, by leaving gaps between the words and adding some full stops. The children could then mark where they feel the full stops should go, and then rewrite the passage in the space provided. In pairs, they should read aloud each other's work, stopping when they reach a full stop. (The teacher may need to demonstrate this.) The children should tell each other whether the full stops are in the right places. The teacher will then need to check the work for accuracy.

Copymaster 104 (Capitals and full stops)
The children need to learn that sentences begin with a capital letter. Also point out that 'I' is always a capital letter, and special names (proper nouns) always start with a capital letter. They should look for these conventions when reading. Demonstrate where capitals and full stops should appear in the first two or three sentences on the copymaster. Then, ask the children to rewrite the sentences correctly.

Copymaster 105 (Read aloud)
Organise the children into pairs, and ask them to read the passage aloud. They will soon see that the writer has not left the reader any instructions as to how it should be read – that is, the full stops and capital letters are missing. In pairs, the children could read through and punctuate the piece. Pairs should then swap finished versions and read them aloud to see if they 'sound

right'. The teacher may need to check the versions to see if full stops are in the right places. (The children may need reminding that people's names should begin with a capital letter.)

Copymaster 106 (Confused?)
This passage is punctuated incorrectly. It should be read aloud and then proofread by the children. Encourage the children to write a passage with no punctuation or incorrectly used punctuation for a friend to work on.

Copymaster 107 (Names)
This copymaster is designed to reinforce the idea that special names: people, places, months, days of the week, seasons and planets all begin with a capital letter. The children should rewrite the sentences correctly in the spaces provided.

Copymaster 108 (A country tale)
Use this copymaster to revise capital letters and full stops. The passage has no capital letters or full stops. The children should proofread it. They could then check each other's work. Where different decisions have been made, the teacher may wish to focus upon the alternative suggestions, reading them aloud to the class and asking for their opinions.

Copymaster 109 (Questions)
The notion of questions should be introduced to the children orally. Questions demand a reply, they ask for an answer. Play a game where the teacher asks questions or makes statements, and the children have to decide which need a reply and are therefore questions. Show the children what a question mark looks like. They should then proofread the copymaster, deciding if each sentence is a **statement** or a **question**, adding a full stop or question mark accordingly. They must also insert capital letters where appropriate. The sentences could be cut up and sorted into piles – statements or questions. On another sheet of paper, they should write replies to the questions. In pairs, the children could play a game where one child gives a reply and their partner sorts through the pile of questions to find the correct one.

Copymaster 110 ('Wh' words)
The children should be introduced to the idea that there is a set of 'question words' beginning with 'Wh' – who, why, when, where and what. The copymaster needs to be read carefully, and a 'Wh' word inserted at the beginning of each sentence. Question marks should also

be inserted. Ask the children to write answers to the questions in order to explore how the choice of 'Wh' word affects their meanings. In pairs, they should ask each other the questions and see if both their sets of replies work.

Copymaster 111 (Crazy questions)

The children should work in pairs. The first child writes a question, starting with the word given, complete with question mark. They then fold the paper to hide the question. Their partner writes an answer to the unseen question and folds the paper, and so on. This game can produce hilarious results, as well as high-lighting the fact that questions and statements are demarcated in different ways. Suggest that one child writes a series of questions about a subject, for example, 'Five questions I would like to ask a mirror'. Their partner should provide imaginative answers. Read these questions and answers to prompt the children:

> Questions I would like to ask a mermaid.
> Why do you sing so sweetly?
> I sing sweetly to trap sailors,
> like wasps to the jam they fly.
> Where is Neptune's palace?
> Neptune's palace is found
> in the heart-beat of a starfish.

Copymaster 112 (Gifts)

This sheet could be used at Christmas-time or for work relating to any celebration when gifts are given. The children should write answers to the questions on the copymaster. Encourage them to provide unusual, magical answers. For example:

I bring you the gift of life.

Where did you find it?
I found it chuckling in the hay,
on a Christmas day, long ago.

When did you capture it?
I caught it when the world
was waking up from a deep sleep.

What was it doing?
It span a thread of time
across the window of eternity.

Who stood on guard?
There was a man dressed in gold,
so old that he was not there.

Why did you steal it?
I stole it to save
your heart from withering.

Copymaster 113 (The Great Yessir)

For each item on the list the children should invent a question to ask the Great Yessir, who knows all that there is to know about the universe! They should ask questions that are a little unusual. For instance: Clock, why do you have a heart-beat? Mirror, when will I meet my twin? Key, where did you find so many locks? Others in the class should try to answer the questions.

Copymaster 114 (Spot the capital)

This copymaster should be introduced with a quick recap of when to use capital letters. The children should begin by circling or underlining the words on the copymaster that need a capital letter. Having spotted the 'capital letter words', they should use all of them in a letter to an imaginary friend. This should provide an opportunity for them to check their own writing for capital letters used correctly. It will also remind them how to lay out a standard letter.

Copymaster 115 (Passport)

Some of the answers to the passport questions will begin with a capital letter. The children could bring in photographs of themselves to complete their passports.

Copymaster 116 (Commas and lists)

This copymaster introduces the idea that commas are used in a list to demarcate the various items. However, a comma is not needed for the final item before the word 'and'. Demonstrate how to write a list in front of the children. Encourage them to use the copymaster to make up funny lists. They should check each other's work. Draw their attention to commas in their own reading and writing.

Copymaster 117 (Lists)

This copymaster can be used to reinforce the skill of writing a list. The children could proofread the lists created and check each other's work.

Copymaster 118 (Name game)

This copymaster should be used to reinforce the idea that initials are written in capital letters. It also supports previous work on adjectives and nouns. The children write down the first two initials of their friends' names in the first column. The second column is for adjectives which begin with these letters, and the third is for nouns beginning with the initial letters. Remind them that the adjective column will contain words that describe the things in the noun column. The combinations can be amusing. Extend the activity by asking the children to use their own initials, and to list all the adjectives and nouns they can – a dictionary will be needed. This produces even stranger results.

Copymaster 119 (Who lives here?)

On this copymaster there is a collection of unusual street names. The children should invent a person who might live in each street, using capital letters for their first name and family name. For example, Soldierly Avenue is where **C**olonel **J**ack **G**unfire lives. Afterwards the children could collect unusual names from maps or a telephone directory. *The Guinness Book of Records* may be useful for investigating odd names.

Copymaster 120 (Funny folk)

This is a list of names taken from 'The Denham Tracts' (1892). It lists some of the folk-creatures and people who had stories told about them. Ask the children to invent a sentence for each 'character', and to write them in the space provided. They should aim to make each sentence alive and interesting by choosing their ideas, adjectives and verbs carefully. Of course each character's name needs to begin with a capital letter. The children could then choose one of the characters to write a story about, or they could create a diary entry or letter 'written' by the character.

Copymaster 121 (Abbreviation)

This copymaster should be read aloud. The children should write what the initials stand for at the base of the copymaster. Draw their attention to the fact that initials of titles, names and organisations have capital letters. The children could collect more abbreviations and find out their meanings.

Copymaster 122 (Teacher terror)

This passage could be used to revise capital letters and full stops. The children should proofread and correct it. They should then check each other's work.

Copymaster 123 (Criminal full stops)

In this passage the full stops and capital letters are in the wrong places. To begin with, the passage should be read aloud as it stands, to make the point that the full stops have been used incorrectly. The children should then proofread the passage.

Copymaster 124 (Letters missing)

The children should write out each sentence (on the copymaster) without the contracted form – so **It's** becomes **It is**. Explain that in speech we often miss letters out of words, for example, don't, can't. When we do this in writing we use an apostrophe to show where the missing letter/s should be. The children should collect examples of contractions from their reading books and list them. They could write the full form beside each one. Remember to point out that **it's** is the contracted form of **it is**, but **its** (possessive) has no apostrophe.

Copymaster 125 (Apostrophes)

Introduce the idea of the 'possessive' – where an apostrophe is used to indicate ownership. The children will need to distinguish between an 's'-ending that indicates a plural and one that indicates ownership. This can be demonstrated by turning the words in a sentence round to show if there is the notion of belonging. For example, Jill cleaned the parrot's cage – the cage of the parrot. If you can use the word **of**, then an apostrophe is needed. The children should rewrite each sentence and insert an apostrophe in the appropriate position. Then, explore what happens if the words are plural, and show them how the apostrophe comes after the complete word. So, if there were three parrots, the example would read, Jill cleaned the three parrots' cage. Ask the children to rewrite the other sentences using plurals.

Copymaster 126 (Types of sentence)

Discuss how sentences fit into three basic categories – commands, questions or statements. Call out different types of sentences to see if the children can identify which type they are. Demonstrate how statements use a full stop, questions use a question mark and commands use an exclamation mark. Explain that this shows the reader how to read the sentence. The copymaster should be proofread and the relevant symbol ticked.

Copymaster 127 (Speech)

Use this copymaster to introduce speech marks, and for the children to practise identifying different types of sentences. The children should draw a balloon from the character around what they actually say. They should then rub out most of the balloon, to leave a fragment either side of the speech – to show where speech marks are written. The speech marks are like a hat or a roof to cover what is being said.

Show the children how to write speech marks correctly, and how they are written outside of any other punctuation, for example, "Stop what you are doing!" The copymaster should be proofread. The children could then compare versions. Discuss any common errors.

Copymaster 128 (Speech marks)

The children should be encouraged to examine the ways in which writers use speech marks, and practise using them in their own work. They could write imaginary conversations which take place at a bus stop, in a playground and at home.

To complete the copymaster, the children should underline what is actually said in each sentence. Speech marks should then be inserted in the appropriate places. Draw the children's attention to how a comma is used before the word 'said' (or its equivalent). There is a space below each sentence for it to be copied out correctly.

Copymaster 129 (Knock, knock)

The children should copy the format provided to write their own 'knock, knock' jokes. The copymasters could then be collected and stapled together to make a 'knock, knock' collection for all to read. The names at the bottom of the copymaster are all used in popular 'knock, knock' jokes. Can the children invent jokes which include them?

Copymaster 130 (Paragraphs)

This copymaster needs to be proofread. It also needs to be divided into paragraphs. Do not attempt to introduce paragraphs until the child is well-established at a level appropriate for a confident Junior. Explain that a paragraph indicates when a writer is moving on to a new subject. It divides the writing up into sections. Often when a new idea or action begins, or when there is a timeshift in the writing, a paragraph is deployed. The children should use a coloured pencil to mark where they think paragraphs might be used to provide a break for the reader. The versions should be read aloud, leaving a long pause for the paragraphs breaks to see if they make sense.

Copymaster 131 (Mucking about)

The children could write their own 'mucking about' poem. Wherever possible, the children should be given access to word processing or desktop publishing facilities.

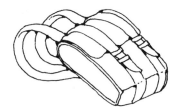

Full stops

onceuponatimetherewerethreelittlepigstheylivedwiththeirmummyin

alargehouseonedaysheIsaidtothemthatitwastimeforthemtogointothe

worldandseektheirfortunesothelittlepigspackedaknapsackeachand

setofftoseewhattheycouldfind

Copymaster 103

Capitals and full stops

1. this is the first day of term

2. look at the fish in the pond

3. here comes the milkman

4. i like to go fishing with mum

5. the cow is happy in the field

6. lorries make a lot of noise

7. ants can walk up walls

8. it is fun to make your own bread

9. this is a picture of my sister

10. susie likes to read books

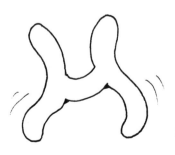

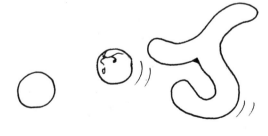

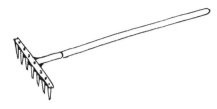 **Read aloud**

at the bottom of the garden janet's father had a shed he kept his

gardening tools in there janet was not allowed to go into the shed one

day she heard a noise from the shed she went down to the bottom

of the garden and looked through the window she could not see

anything she pushed open the door it was very dark inside a spider

had spun a web a mouse ran for safety janet stared at the mouse it

was not a tiny mouse it was the size of a cat it sat up and stared

back at her

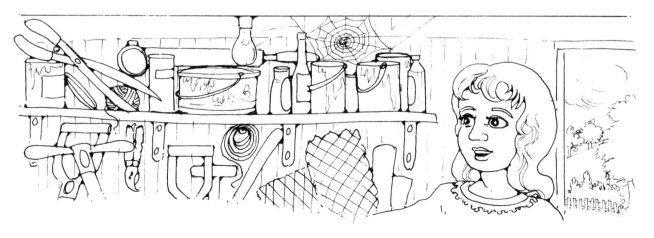

Copymaster 105

Confused?

It was a dark, and wintery night when. tom heard a baby Crying he

crept out of his. house he ran Down the street in the end. he found

the baby It was on the steps. of the church tom picked Up the baby.

he carried it home he fed. it on warm milk and bread. he wrapped it

up warmly he. sat in front of the Fire he wondered what He should

do. in the morning he took his dog. And the baby down to the police

station

Names

1. i am going to visit my friend in london

2. jane and janet are my best friends

3. we want to name our new pet gerbil timmy

4. on monday it will be the first day of april

5. this year we are going to hastings for our holiday

6. mars is a planet

7. i love eating mars bars

8. jake and i are going to france with the school

9. this tuesday is the last day of may

10. i cannot help liking bill

Name _____

A country tale

this is a story about a red-haired thief whose name was digger digger lived on the edge of the village he had five children and he named them after the days of the week his favourite son was called monday his favourite daughter was called friday one morning he asked tuesday to take the cow to highbury town where john lived digger went to fetch the cow from john john kept the cow in his field in the months of april and may

Name _____

Questions

1. is this a question

2. have you seen my new bicycle

3. this is my gerbil called frank

4. is this the way to school

5. that dog is going to bite you

6. do you want to come and look

7. on friday kay comes home

8. show me how to mend it

9. will you give me a sweet

10. can we come in

'Wh' words

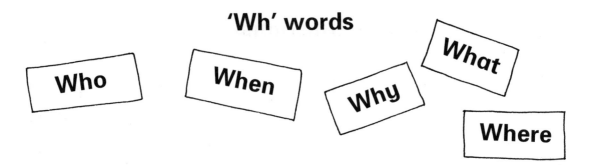

Who   When   Why   What   Where

are you staring at the budgie

are the keys to the door

are the soldiers singing

is that terrible smell

is going to feed the pig

are you making porridge

 # Crazy questions

Why
Where
Who
What
When

Gifts

I bring you the gift of life.

Where did you find it?

When did you capture it?

What was it doing?

Who stood on guard?

Why did you steal it?

The Great Yessir

A mirror

A key

A hilltop

Silence

On your birthday

Your parents

Diamonds

The North wind

Spot the capital

monday	june
sasha	carpenter
pig	friday
bread	woman
summer	butterfly
joe	america
i	july
wednesday	they
april	mug
ted	clock
scotland	australia
tina	wish
christmas	bee
we	august
month	thursday
ireland	us
carrot	trouble

Passport

Name?

Name of street?

Name of town?   Favourite TV programme?

Name of county?   Favourite film?

Friend's name?   Favourite book?

Best day of the week?   Favourite author?

Commas and lists

In the emu's beak I found

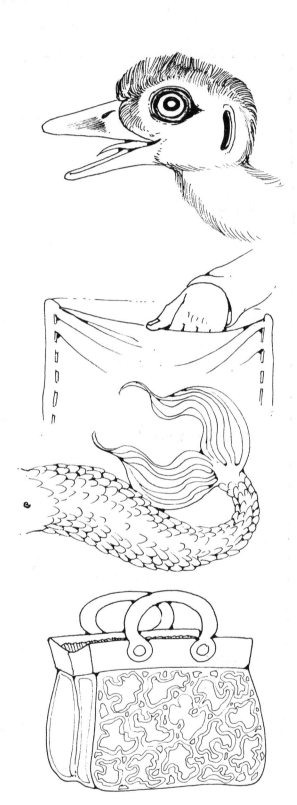

In the giant's pocket I found

In a mermaid's purse I found

In my teacher's bag I found

Name _____

 **Lists**

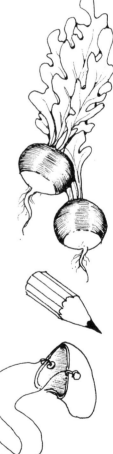

1. I went to the zoo and saw a lion a hippo a kangaroo

   and a monkey.

2. I went shopping and bought a can of beans a cucumber

   some beans and a packet of pasta.

3. In the salad I put some lettuce a tomato cucumber

   radishes and celery.

4. In my pocket I keep an old hanky a piece of gum a

   pencil some sweet wrappers and a false nose.

5. I like to play with my toys jigsaw puzzles my dolls

   and my brother.

Copymaster 117

Name game

Initials	Adjective	Noun
P.C.	Pink	Cabbage

Who lives here?

Longtooth Street

Old Man's Lane

Weary Wood

Saddle Ridge

Gossipworth Park

Soldierly Avenue

Elegant Towers

Thunderous Flats

Dimlit Block

Proudsfoot Parade

Chucklinbury Circus

Giggleswick High Street

Slim Alley

Sweetly Way

Short Cutting

Name _____

Funny folk

Boogle Bugbear   Shellcoat   Robin-Goodfellow   Mum-Poker
Tom-Tumbler   Hobby-Lanthorn   Snapdragon   Hob-thrust
Jinny-Burnt-Tail   Clabbernapper   Thrummy-Cap

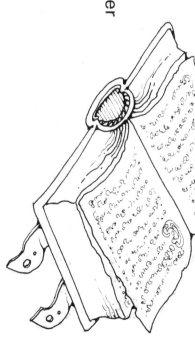

Abbreviation

Col Sanders looked the C.I.D. officer in the eye and began to talk.
"Well, I was on the M25 in the B.M.W. on my way down to visit my
Mrs. She was staying with the Rev. who married us in a little C of E
at Ryde. I broke down and couldn't get in touch with the A.A. or the
R.A.C. I wasn't sure how many km I had driven. I didn't know if it
was a.m. or p.m. I'd forgotten my money and didn't even know the
telephone number. I thought I was stuck when a S.R.N. pulled up in
a V.W. and took me to the nearest B.R. station. I told her I couldn't
pay her but she said that I could leave an I.O.U. in the R.S.P.C.A. or
N.S.P.C.C. charity box.

Teacher terror

mr badgrump stormed into the class class 3 sat and trembled

they knew that they were in trouble it had started out as an

ordinary thursday usually thursdays were better than

wednesdays because on thursdays they had miss

smileyface for music she was a vision of twinkling

smiles compared to mr badgrump mr badgrump was

the terror of st peters primary school indeed he was the

terror of the little town of chipping sudsoap there were

many adults in the town who crossed to the

other side of the road when they saw their old

teacher approaching mr badgrump's eyes flickered

round the room nobody moved the classroom was

quiet the silence was broken as the door swung open

and in walked harry dumberry just back

from his summer holidays in edinburgh

Criminal full stops

last night i had the strangest. of dreams i was

standing. at the edge of The classroom. and a small man

was peering at our books. he had taken some of the books. off

the shelves he was. shaking the pages above a sack and

all the full Stops were falling. into the sack he turned. around

and winked at me i stared at him. as he pulled another

book from the shelf and began to gently blow. on the

Pages full stops scattered. on to the floor like a thousand tiny

Black pin-pricks. he puffed again and all the commas shot

off the page and Lay. on the ground like tadpoles. he winked

at me and i found that i could not speak. he began to

walk towards me. clutching his bag i was. terrified he just

smiled and walked Off i scrabbled on the floor and began to

stick the full stops back. into the Books some might

have been put in the wrong Places i am not sure

   **Letters missing**

1. It's my turn to read from the book.

2. We're not going to give you any.

3. I've got all the strawberries I need.

4. You'll be sorry for saying that.

5. I'd imagine that the goblins will return.

6. You weren't to blame for what happened.

7. You don't have to wear that mask.

8. I wouldn't do that if I were you.

9. Where's the kitchen in this house?

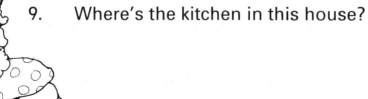 

Copymaster 124

Name _____

Apostrophes

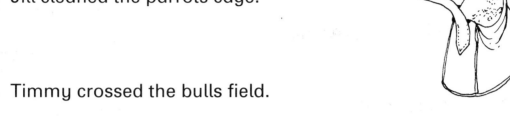

1. Jill cleaned the parrots cage.

2. Timmy crossed the bulls field.

3. Jolie went to find the horses food bag.

4. I kept away from the emus beak.

5. We looked for the soldiers gun.

6. There was soup on the waiters shoes.

7. The Indian longed for the bisons freedom.

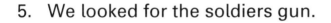

Types of sentence

 It is a fine painting

 Ouch, that hurt

./?/! Don't you dare do that

 Is there enough petrol to get home

./?/! There are thousands of seals in the swimming pool

./?/! Where did they come from

 I haven't got any idea

 You could run across those fields

 That is a very ugly baby

 Why didn't you ask for a tissue

./?/! Those flowers are yellow and orange

Speech

Give me a kiss

What is that frog doing there

Come back

I'm tired

Can I have my ball back

Speech marks

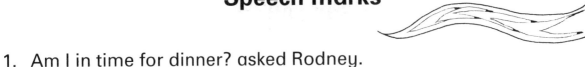

1. Am I in time for dinner? asked Rodney.

2. That is beautiful, said Miranda.

3. Let us have some chocolates now, muttered Steven.

4. Fiona said, This is my new puppy.

5. Jason replied, He is an Alsatian and they bite.

6. Kelly whispered, This is a secret.

7. If you listen, whispered Jodie, I will tell you.

8. Hold my arm, said the Knight, and you will not fall.

9. I cannot, replied Joanna, I am falling asleep.

10. Stop! yelled the butcher.

Knock, knock

"Knock, knock."   "Who's there?"   "Sherwood."

"Sherwood who?"   "Sherwood like to kiss you."

Ivor   Celeste   Cook   Felix   Doctor   Boo   Lena   Arthur

Paragraphs

when kelly woke that morning the sun was shining down she yawned and sat up in bed it was her big day the schools first match against dudley lane primary school all that morning she couldnt concentrate on her work several times miss davies had to tell her to get on with her work sorry miss said kelly but i was thinking about this afternoon at the end of the day the class went home and kelly ran down to get changed soon the game would begin everyone was very excited and their was a lot of noise will you lot hurry up said miss davies once the game had started there was no time to chatter kelly played as fast and as hard as she could her mum stood on the touch-line with little jodie and they cheered as hard as they could

Mucking about

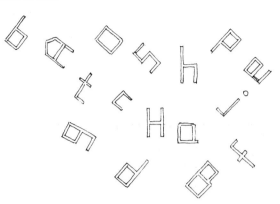

i liKe to MuCk about

with LANGUAGE –

O.K.?????

If you want to you can do silly things.

Youcanrunitalltogether

ooooooorrrrrrrrr uuuuuussssssssseeeeeeee too many letterssssssssss.

... I. k.n.o.w. a. b.o.y. w.h.o. p.u.t.s.

a full stop in after every l.e.t.t.e.r.

Some days I like to do a row

of ???????????????????????????????

BeCaUsE they are like fishing hooks.

I think I'm hooked on them!

My

favourite

is

the

!!!!!!!!!!!

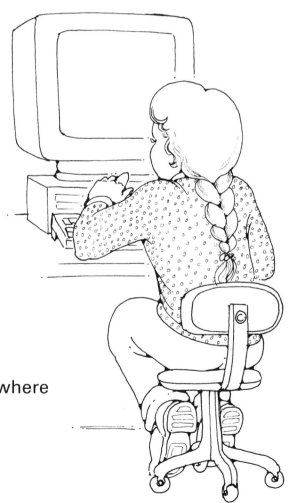

I' also' p'ut in' thes'e one's i'n the a'ir

it bre'aks the wo'rds up ni'cely.

The worst are ''the speaking marks'' – where

they go

,''not even my computer can tell me.

Pie Corbett

RECORD KEEPING

This section provides a quick checklist for the work that has been introduced to a class by this book. I have included two 'quick reminder' sheets with basic descriptions of terminology and punctuation functions. The definitions provided will be sufficient for teachers working with young children.

Copymaster 132 (Class checklist)
This copymaster could be used as a reference sheet for recording the children's development in their use of punctuation. Mark the boxes provided as follows:

✔ indicates introduced to.

✗ indicates the child sometimes uses this aspect accurately.

■ indicates the child is accurate in their use of this aspect.

Copymasters 133 and 134 (The quick reminder)
These copymasters could be used as a speedy reminder of terms for colleagues or children. However, more complex definitions can be found in books quoted in the booklist. For instance, the *L.I.N.C. Materials for Professional Development* contains a useful glossary while *All About English* provides working explanations for Key Stage 3 children.

Class checklist

Child's name	Paragraphs	Exclamation marks	Speech marks	Apostrophes	Commas	Question marks	Capital letters	Full stops

The quick reminder

GRAMMATICAL TERMS
These are terms used to describe and name different words in writing. It is useful to know and use these terms when discussing reading and writing.

NOUNS
These are the **names** of people, places, objects, creatures, ideas and feelings. They tell us what a sentence is about.

PROPER NOUNS
These are the **special names** of people, places, days of the week, months, seasons and planets. They all begin with a capital letter.

ADJECTIVES
These words **describe nouns**, for example, red, tiny, frail.

VERBS
These are **doing** words, providing the sentence with action. Verbs, for example, run, leap, whisper, listen, bring a sentence to life.

ADVERBS
These are **added to verbs** to tell us more about them. They often end in **ly**, for example, slowly and quickly.

PREPOSITIONS
These words show us the position of nouns in a sentence, for example, on, in and underneath.

CONJUNCTIONS
These **join** or **connect** parts of sentences together, such as: and, then, but, because and so on.

ARTICLES
This is the smallest group of words: a, an, the. An is used before a word that starts with a vowel.

PRONOUNS
Pronouns take the place of a noun, and are useful to avoid repetition. They include: I, you, he, she, it, we, they, mine, him, her, us, them, theirs, ours, yours.

Copymaster 133

The quick reminder

PUNCTUATION
Punctuation is a convention used by writers to give readers instructions.

FULL STOPS
These are used at the end of sentences that are statements.

CAPITAL LETTERS
These are used to begin sentences, proper nouns, and for special initials. I, when used as a word, is always a capital letter.

COMMAS
Symbols used to separate items in a list, and to indicate brief pauses in sentences.

APOSTROPHES
These show where letters are missing in **contracted** words, such as don't. They are used to show **possession** , for example, this is Tom's coat.

Note:
1. In plurals, the apostrophe is placed after the **s**. For example, the girls' sweets.
2. **It's** means **it is**, whereas **its** is used for the **possessive**.

SPEECH MARKS
These are used to indicate what has actually been said. They are sometimes called inverted commas.

Note:
1. Punctuation marks should fall inside the final set of speech marks. For example, ''It is good'', said John – is not correct, whereas – ''It is good,'' said John – is correct.
2. A comma is used before said or its equivalent.

EXCLAMATION MARKS
These are placed at the end of a command or exclaiming sentence.

PARAGRAPHS
These divide writing up into sections, and are used to denote a shift in time, a new event, or a different aspect of a topic.

Copymaster 134